The Ultimate Ice Cream Cake Book

The Ultimate ICE CREAM CAKE BOOK

50 FUN RECIPES TO SATISFY ANY SWEET TOOTH

KELLY MIKOLICH

PHOTOGRAPHY BY MARIJA VIDAL

ROCKRIDGE PRESS

Interior and Cover Designer: Erin Yeung
Art Producer: Sue Bischofberger
Editor: Natasha Yglesias
Production Editor: Rachel Taenzler

Photography © 2019 Marija Vidal. Food styling by Elisabet der Nederlanden.

Author photo courtesy of Barbara Alanis at One Day Photography.

ISBN: Print 978-1-64152-726-2 | eBook 978-1-64152-727-9

R0

To my momma and daddy, who are responsible for my love of ice cream cakes. And for being the most amazing parents ever, of course!

Contents

Introduction

Hi friends! Well, we might not exactly be friends just yet, but I'm hoping as you work your way through this book, you'll feel like I'm right there in the kitchen alongside you. My name is Kelly, and I'm a recipe developer and blogger at Kelly Lynn's Sweets and Treats. Baking is my passion and learning how to make delicious desserts from scratch is my hobby. Making ice cream cakes from scratch is so much better than using a boxed cake mix and store-bought ice cream. Homemade is fresher, *and* you get to control the ingredients you use—and because this girl loves her some ice cream cake, I just had to write an entire cookbook dedicated to it.

My love of ice cream cakes dates back to my childhood. My family celebrated birthdays with ice cream cakes, and every year I got to pick out the flavors I wanted for mine. This was the ultimate treat—and secretly my favorite part of my birthday. Now, as an adult, I put my love of baking to use by creating ice cream cakes of every kind.

If you're reading this, I'm assuming you share my passion for ice cream cakes (or at the very least, eating them). This cookbook is for you. I want you to have fun while making these recipes, so be creative or make substitutions if you want—whatever feels right to you. Have a specific party theme? Use a special shaped pan and creative decorations for your ice cream cake. While I've included suggestions for decorations, feel free to change them up to make the cakes your own.

The ice cream cakes here are made completely from scratch. But never fear, I'll take you step by step through each recipe and explain the best way to construct your ice cream cake. Plus, I'll share tips and tricks along the way to ensure that you have sweet success.

Grab your apron (and your ice cream maker, of course) and let's make some ice cream cakes!

A Tasty Love Affair

Let's take a trip back in time to 1990-something. There was little ten-year-old Kelly, anxiously waiting to dive into her birthday cake. Her hands rested on her chin as she sat at the family table—anxious to blow out the candles so she could devour a huge slice of luscious, moist cake layered with creamy ice cream.

While I may not remember the presents I got for my tenth birthday, I do remember the chocolate chip ice cream cake. It was the perfect birthday dessert made with flavors I chose myself. Parties and presents were fun, but having a customized ice cream cake was always my favorite part of the celebration. Fast forward to today and I'm the one who gets the pleasure of being the baker who creates the desserts for all our family celebrations! There's nothing more satisfying than creating something special, something that never fails to bring a smile to those you love.

Nothing says *celebration* like an ice cream cake, and in my mind, no birthday party—or any kind of celebration for that matter—is complete without it. Combining cake and ice cream gives you the ultimate pairing of textures: the moistness of cake with the creaminess of ice cream. It's the perfect bite. Plus, it's so much easier to serve and clean up as a whole, rather than dishing the ice cream out separately. That's the mom in me talking (less dishes, less mess).

I'm all about homemade desserts, and there are so many benefits to making your own rather than buying one. I don't know if you've been into your local ice cream shop lately, but they charge an arm and a leg for their ice cream cakes! Why fork out all that cash when you can make your own—one that tastes a million times better? People will be seriously impressed, and you'll see that making ice cream cake isn't that hard. In fact, it's really fun to do. I enjoy being able to craft my dessert into whatever shape I want. The options are endless and always sweet, so join me on this journey to create ice cream cake desserts that will satisfy your inner child and create lasting memories.

CHAPTER ONE

Ice Cream Cake 101

Let's learn some ice cream cake basics. In this chapter, I'll walk you through different ice creams and cakes, as well as the different types of equipment you'll need to get started on your tasty adventure.

I Scream

Let's talk ice cream bases, the liquid mixture of ingredients churned and transformed into ice cream. There are four main ice cream bases:

The custard base is going to be "richer" because it includes egg yolks, cream, and sugar. You cook it on the stovetop, cool it, and then put it into the ice cream machine to work its magic. You have to be careful not to scramble the eggs while you cook the base, and once made, the mixture must chill in the fridge before churning. The payoff for all this hard work is a rich and creamy ice cream. I like using this base in cakes where the standout flavor is the ice cream itself.

The Philadelphia-style base is made with just cream, sugar, and any flavors we add. The fat comes entirely from the cream. Some recipes may call for the base being cooked first (like the custard base) in order to dissolve the sugar, but you could skip that step and go straight to churning. Philadelphia-style ice cream is smooth and less rich than the custard base. It's usually best eaten the same day it's made, but I have a trick to help extend the freshness of this ice cream: Add dry milk powder to the base. Okay . . . I guess I just gave away the secret, but we *are* friends now, right? I like this base for scooping on top of cupcakes and in cake rolls, times when I want the cake flavors to outshine the ice cream.

The egg-free base—you guessed it—doesn't have any eggs. This base is thickened with cornstarch and cream cheese. It's rich, smooth, and allows the flavors of the ice cream to truly shine. It's much easier to make than the classic custard base because we don't have to deal with eggs. It's a great base to use for boozy ice creams because it tends to freeze rock solid.

The no-churn base is probably my favorite of all the ice cream bases because it's so easy to make. No ice cream machine is required, so it was the first type of homemade ice cream I ever made. I was absolutely amazed you could make such a creamy ice cream without a machine. All you need is a stand mixer and two ingredients: cream and sweetened condensed milk. Use your choice of flavoring and mix-ins, then pop the ice cream into the freezer. You can use this base in any of the ice cream cake recipes in this book.

Ice Cream Makers

The recipes in this book are based on a 1½-quart electric ice cream maker, except for the no-churn ice cream recipes (for which no machine is required). Always follow the manufacturer instructions on your ice cream maker, as they may differ from brand to brand. Some recipes may have to be adjusted based on the type of ice cream machine you're using. The amount of churning time may vary among manufacturers and it also depends on the size of the ice cream machine used. Freezing times and ingredient measurements should be the same.

I use a Cuisinart ICE-21R Frozen Yogurt, Ice Cream & Sorbet Maker for the recipes in this book because it's a brand that I trust. I have several Cuisinart appliances and they've all stood the test of time. Also, the price is fairly moderate.

I'm happy to see that the days of ice cream machines requiring ice and salt to churn are long gone. Say goodbye to those ice cream balls you have to shake violently forever in order to yield a tiny amount of ice cream. Buy a fully automatic machine that allows you to simply pour the mixture into the machine, press a button, and make *magic*! Delicious, creamy ice cream in just 20 minutes. Bonus: Cleanup is a breeze.

If, however, you don't plan on buying an ice cream maker any time soon, remember that you can always make a no-churn version of any of the ice creams in this book.

You Scream

Ice cream cakes were originally invented during the Victorian era. Advances in freezing technology made frozen desserts more accessible and allowed for chefs to create more intricate frozen desserts—such as bombes, a dessert consisting of biscuits and cream layered into decorative molds with fruit. In this book, you'll find a variety of ice cream cake creations, from layered cakes to Bundt cakes and more! I've done my best to think outside the proverbial ice cream carton and come up with recipes that are beyond the average imagination but also easy to make. My aim is to create show-stopping cakes that are a yummy addition to any celebration.

Each chapter has a variety of styles of ice cream cakes, so you'll have options on what works best for your particular celebration.

Layered cake—layers of cake and ice cream covered in frosting or ganache—is probably the most common ice cream cake out there. This is the type I grew up eating, though the ones in this book take it to a whole new level. The flavors range from over-the-top chocolate ice cream cakes to fruit-filled wonders. The layered cake is a great option for feeding a large crowd, too.

Cake rolls—also known as Swiss rolls—are believed to have originated in Europe, possibly in England, and worked their way to the United States in the 1850s thanks to New York bakers, who imported goods from Europe and France. Cake rolls are usually filled with frosting before rolling, but in this book we use ice cream instead—a method that has become fairly common in the ice cream cake world. This is a great cake to make ahead of time and store in the freezer until you need it. They might look intimidating to make, but they are actually pretty easy. And don't worry—if your cake cracks, spread a little frosting to cover it. Frosting fixes everything.

Cupcakes were invented way back in the 1700s and were called "number cakes"—light cakes baked in cups. When you think about cupcakes, you probably don't think *ice cream* cupcakes, but I'm going to change your mind! Instead of frosting on top, we'll use a scoop of ice cream. This is a fun way to serve up cake and ice cream in individual portions, plus I love that I can make the cupcakes and the ice cream well ahead of time to freeze until it's time to party.

Cheesecake is believed to have originated in ancient Greece, where it was served to the first Olympic athletes to give them energy. Now that's my kind of energy food! What's not to love about the creamy, tangy flavor of a cheesecake? The majority of the cheesecakes in this book are no-bake cheesecakes, which work best when layered with ice cream. The addition of ice cream to a cheesecake results in the ultimate creamy, decadent ice cream cake. I promise you, that first bite will have you wanting more.

Bundt cakes became popular in the 1950s and 1960s after Nordic Ware began producing a style of cast aluminum mold they trademarked as the Bundt pan. Now you can buy the pans in a wide variety of shapes and designs. Just add ice cream and it's a complete dessert. Bundt cakes are great to make ahead and freeze, too.

I included a few other fun twists on cake as well. There's definitely an ice cream cake for everyone in this book.

Prep Time

Some planning and preparation go into constructing ice cream cakes, so it's best to read through the entire recipe prior to making it.

If you're making ice cream in an ice cream maker, it's important to completely freeze the ice cream freezer bowl for at least one day prior to making it. No-churn ice cream is soft when it's made, so it needs more time than other ice creams—several hours in the freezer—to become frozen. Most of the recipes in the book call for the ice cream bases to be chilled overnight and then the ice cream to be frozen overnight, so you should start making the ice cream two days before you plan to eat it. Below are the minimum times for chilling and freezing.

Chilling and Freezing Times for Ice Cream Bases

TYPE	CHILLING TIME	FREEZING TIME
Custard-style base	4 hours	4 hours
Philadelphia-style base	4 hours	1 hour
Egg-free base	0 hours	1 hour
No-churn base	0 hours	6 hours

Most of the recipes in this cookbook are made in stages, because freshly baked cake needs to chill before layering with ice cream (unless you like ice cream soup). Because the different layers of each recipe are made separately, you can make some layers ahead of time, which saves you from spending an entire day in the kitchen.

When it comes time to assemble the layers of cake and ice cream, trust in the directions of the recipe. I tried to make the assembly of the cake the easiest (and most fun) part of creating your ice cream cake. Just make sure you have enough room in your freezer for your ice cream cake once it's all constructed.

We All Scream

You're almost ready to get started. But let's check to make sure you have what you need in the kitchen.

Tools and Equipment

Here are a few of the key pieces of equipment needed to make these ice cream cakes come to life:

Baking pans: We use baking pans not only to bake the cakes, but for freezing the ice cream (that way the ice cream and cake layers are the same size when it's time to layer them together). I suggest having several 8-inch round cake pans and several 8-inch square pans. I prefer nonstick steel baking pans for both baking and freezing.

Blender: This appliance is really helpful for mixing up ice cream bases and blending shakes. Nothing fancy needed here, just your average blender will do the job.

Bundt pan: You should have a good-quality, standard Bundt pan that holds at least 10 cups of batter, in whatever design you fancy. I prefer cast aluminum Bundt pans because I think they bake more evenly.

Donut pan: These are inexpensive pans used to make baked, rather than fried, donuts. Baking them is much easier than frying, and healthier, too.

Ice cream storage containers: I have several reusable plastic ice cream containers with silicone lids. If the ice cream we're making doesn't need to be a certain size for a layer, these containers are the best way to store ice cream until you're ready to use it.

Offset spatulas: I own several offset spatulas in different sizes. They make frosting cakes easy-peasy. I also use offset spatulas for spreading ice cream when making cake rolls.

Sieves or fine-mesh strainers: Always a handy baking tool to have in any kitchen. Using a sieve helps produce ice cream that has a smooth texture.

Stand mixer: My KitchenAid stand mixer is probably my most loved appliance. I call for a stand mixer to make the no-churn ice cream, frostings, and cakes in this book, but a hand mixer can also be used. A stand mixer is definitely worth the investment. I thought I would never use mine when I got it as a present from my husband, but I use it almost every day and it's become like a second set of hands in the kitchen. Use the paddle attachment for whipping and beating. Use the whisk attachment for whisking.

Ingredients

Recipes only taste as good as the quality of the ingredients. High-quality, fresh ingredients play a key role in the taste of any finished product. Every recipe here features simple, all-natural ingredients you probably already have on hand or can easily find in your local supermarket.

Eggs: I'm lucky to get farm-fresh eggs from my sister's farm. I even help feed her chickens! If you're buying eggs in the grocery store, there are many options to choose from—organic, brown, white, cage-free, pasteurized—and any of these varieties will work. The recipes in this cookbook all use large, grade AA chicken eggs.

Fresh cream and whole milk: High-quality cream and milk with a high fat content are needed to make a rich and creamy ice cream. Use whatever brand you prefer or have available to you—it's your choice whether to buy organic. The taste of cream and milk can vary depending on the brand, due to different climates and diets of the cows. To me, freshness is what is most important.

Sugar: Superfine granulated sugar will give you the creamiest ice cream.

For the cakes, I often call for ingredients "at room temperature" because they will mix together more easily and be less prone to curdling.

Remember to check the expiration dates on your pantry items. If expired, ingredients such as flour, cocoa powder, baking powder, and baking soda may cause your cakes to not rise properly. There's a variety of ice cream cakes in this cookbook, so if there's an ingredient you can't find, or have an allergy to, switch it up. Make these cakes your own way with the ingredients you love.

Life gets busy. I get it. Maybe you don't have time to make homemade ice cream or homemade cake. If you're in a pinch, use a high-quality store-bought ice cream or cake mix. Häagen-Dazs makes great ice cream in a variety of flavors. I also love Ben & Jerry's for all their crazy, fun flavors, which would work well in any of these recipes. Need a shortcut for the cake-baking portion? Betty Crocker and Duncan Hines are my go-to cake mixes when I'm in a hurry. I love Betty Crocker for their brownie mix and cookie pouches, too. A way to add a homemade touch to any boxed cake, brownie, or cookie mix is to add a splash of vanilla or a pinch of nutmeg before baking.

Storage Tips

Before getting started on your ice cream cake creation, clean out that freezer! Throw out anything unrecognizable and eat up all those leftovers. You need to have ample space for all the components, as well as room for the finished cake, fully constructed.

Custard ice cream will stay fresh in the freezer for up to 2 weeks.

No-churn ice cream will stay fresh in the freezer for up to 3 weeks. Pressing a piece of plastic wrap directly on the ice cream will help prevent ice crystals from forming.

Philadelphia-style and **eggless ice cream** are best eaten within 2 days.

Once the cake is constructed, make sure it's tightly wrapped in plastic wrap and stored in a freezer set on the coldest setting. When storing smaller cakes (leftover slices, cupcakes, etc.), place them in a freezer-proof zipper-top bag, which will extend the life of your desserts.

Ice cream cakes are best eaten within 3 to 5 days of construction.

Ice cream cheesecakes are best eaten within 2 to 3 days.

Mint Chocolate Chip Cake 18

CHAPTER TWO

Chocolate

Mmm . . . *chocolate*. It's considered a classic for a reason. In this chapter, you'll find my dream creations: everything from layered chocolate cakes to ice cream cupcakes—even pancakes! Chocolate makes every-thing better, and a chocolate ice cream cake is always perfect for any celebration. Many of the cakes in this chapter remind me of the ones I grew up eating, and they bring back fond memories. I hope making and sharing these cakes does the same for you.

Triple Chocolate Layer Cake 13

Fudgy Pecan Round Cake 16

Mint Chocolate Chip Cake 18

Epic Chocolate Chip Cookie Ice Cream Cake 20

Giant Ice Cream Sandwich 23

Ultimate Candy Ice Cream Cake 25

Cookies and Cream Ice Cream Cake 28

White Chocolate Cake 30

Chocolate Wonderland Cake 33

Chocolate Malt Madness Cake 35

Chocolate-Hazelnut Ice Cream Cupcakes 38

Neapolitan Ice Cream Shake 40

Red Velvet Celebration Pancakes with
Maple-Cream Cheese Ice Cream 42

Vanilla Roll Cake 44

Spicy Mexican Chocolate Bundt Ice Cream Cake 46

TRIPLE CHOCOLATE LAYER CAKE

· ·

MAKES **8 to 10 Slices** | PREP TIME: **1 hour, plus overnight to chill and 30 minutes to freeze** | COOK TIME: **37 minutes**

Three kinds of chocolate are used in this cake to satisfy the ultimate chocolate lover. I'd also like to call this cake "The Answer to a Bad Day," because if you've had one, what would *you* rather have: chocolate or kale? We both know the answer to that.

For the cake

Nonstick cooking spray

¾ cup plus 2 tablespoons all-purpose flour

¾ cup plus 2 tablespoons granulated sugar

¼ cup plus 2 tablespoons unsweetened cocoa powder

½ teaspoon baking powder

1 teaspoon baking soda

⅛ teaspoon salt

½ cup buttermilk, at room temperature

¼ cup canola oil

1 egg, at room temperature

1 teaspoon vanilla extract

½ cup hot, freshly brewed black coffee

For the ice cream

8 ounces white chocolate, chopped

1 cup French vanilla coffee creamer

⅔ cup granulated sugar

⅛ teaspoon salt

5 egg yolks

1½ teaspoons vanilla extract

2 cups heavy cream

For the ganache

1 cup semisweet chocolate chips, plus more for sprinkling (optional)

½ cup heavy cream

1 tablespoon butter

To make the ice cream

1. Place the white chocolate in a large bowl and set aside. In a medium pot over medium heat, mix together the coffee creamer, sugar, and salt and heat until warm. Remove from the heat.

2. In a medium bowl, whisk together the egg yolks. Slowly whisk the creamer mixture into the egg yolks. Pour the mixture back into the pot and continue to cook over medium heat until thickened.

CONTINUED

3. Using a sieve or a fine-mesh strainer placed over the bowl with the chocolate, pour the hot mixture through the strainer and onto the chocolate. Stir until the chocolate is completely melted. Stir in vanilla extract and cream and let cool for 30 minutes.

4. Cover the bowl with plastic wrap and refrigerate the mixture overnight. Place the bowl from the ice cream maker in the freezer overnight.

5. Pour the chilled ice cream mixture into the ice cream maker and process according to the manufacturer's instructions.

6. Line two 8-inch round cake pans with plastic wrap. Once the ice cream is done churning, pour it evenly into the two pans. Cover the pans with plastic wrap and freeze for 4 to 6 hours.

To make the cake

1. Preheat the oven to 350°F. Line the bottom of an 8-inch round cake pan with parchment paper and spray the pan with cooking spray. Set aside.

2. Sift the dry ingredients into a medium bowl and set aside.

3. In the bowl of a stand mixer, mix together the buttermilk, oil, egg, and vanilla on medium until fully incorporated. Reduce the speed to low and slowly mix in the dry ingredients until incorporated. Slowly pour the hot coffee into the batter, mixing until combined.

4. Remove the bowl from the mixer and use a rubber spatula to ensure the ingredients are incorporated.

5. Pour the batter into the prepared cake pan. Bake for 24 minutes, or until a toothpick inserted into the middle comes out clean. Place the cake on a wire rack to cool.

6. Store in an airtight container at room temperature for up to 2 to 3 days.

To make the ganache

1. In a microwave-safe bowl, add the chocolate chips and pour the heavy cream over them. Add the butter.

2. Microwave in 30-second increments, stopping to stir in between, until the chocolate is melted. Let cool for 15 to 20 minutes before using.

To construct the cake

1. On a cake plate, place the layer of chocolate cake, upside down.

2. Place both layers of white chocolate ice cream on top of the chocolate cake layer. Pour the cooled chocolate ganache on top of the ice cream, allowing it to drip down the sides. Sprinkle with chocolate chips (if using).

3. Place the cake in the freezer to set for 30 minutes before covering tightly with plastic wrap and freezing until ready to serve.

TIP: Adding brewed coffee to the chocolate cake batter enhances the flavor and richness of the chocolate, without making the cake taste like coffee.

FUDGY PECAN ROUND CAKE

MAKES 8 to 10 slices | PREP TIME: 45 minutes, plus overnight to chill and 30 minutes to freeze | COOK TIME: 35 minutes

This ice cream cake is reminiscent of the cakes my dad has requested every year for his birthday. It's the perfect slice of chocolate cake, with chocolate chip ice cream, rich chocolate icing, and toasted pecans, all in one bite. I have the best dad in the world, so I would make this cake for him any day of the year—and help him eat it, too.

For the cake

1 recipe Triple Chocolate Layer Cake (page 13), baked in a parchment-lined 8-inch square baking pan for 25 minutes and cooled

For the ice cream

1½ cups heavy cream

¾ cup whole milk

1 tablespoon vanilla extract

½ cup super fine granulated sugar

⅛ teaspoon salt

½ cup mini chocolate chips

½ cup semi-sweet chocolate chips

For the icing

½ cup unsalted butter

½ cup unsweetened cocoa powder

6 tablespoons evaporated milk

3¾ cups powdered sugar

1½ teaspoons vanilla extract

⅛ teaspoon salt

2 cups toasted pecan pieces

To make the ice cream

1. Place the bowl from the ice cream maker in the freezer overnight.

2. In a medium bowl, whisk together the cream, milk, vanilla, sugar, and salt. Place the mixture in the refrigerator overnight.

3. Line an 8-inch-square baking pan with plastic wrap.

4. Pour the chilled mixture into a 1½-quart ice cream maker and process according to the manufacturer's directions. Five minutes before the ice cream is done churning, pour in the mini chocolate chips and semi-sweet chocolate chips while the machine is still running and let the ice cream finish processing.

5. Pour the ice cream into the prepared pan. Place in the freezer for 4 to 6 hours before using.

To construct the cake

On a cake plate, place the cake upside down. Spread the ice cream in a thick layer over the cake and place back in the freezer.

To make the icing

1. In a medium pot over medium heat, add the butter, cocoa powder, and evaporated milk. Bring the mixture to a boil, whisking occasionally.

2. Add the powdered sugar, vanilla, and salt and whisk continuously for 30 to 60 seconds, or until completely smooth.

3. Remove the cake from the freezer and pour the icing evenly over the top. Sprinkle the toasted pecans over the top.

4. Place the cake in the freezer to set for 30 minutes before covering tightly with plastic wrap and freezing until ready to serve.

5. Store leftovers, tightly covered with plastic wrap, in the freezer for 3 to 5 days.

TIP: Any nut can be substituted for the pecans or left off completely. If not using nuts for the top of the cake, sprinkle the top with semi-sweet chocolate chips to get a "crunchy" texture.

MINT CHOCOLATE CHIP CAKE

· ·

MAKES **8 to 10 slices** | PREP TIME: **30 minutes, plus overnight to chill and 30 minutes to freeze** | COOK TIME: **25 minutes**

Mint chocolate chip ice cream was my favorite growing up. I used to stop by the store on my walk home from school and buy a carton, go home, and proceed to eat almost all of it by myself! To make it even better now, I layer the ice cream on chocolate mint cake. The. Best.

For the cake

Nonstick cooking spray

¾ cup plus 2 tablespoons
  all-purpose flour

¾ cup plus 2 tablespoons
  granulated sugar

¼ cup plus 2 tablespoons unsweetened
  cocoa powder

½ teaspoon baking powder

1 teaspoon baking soda

⅛ teaspoon salt

½ cup buttermilk, at room temperature

¼ cup canola oil

1 egg, at room temperature

1 teaspoon peppermint extract

½ cup hot water

For the no-churn ice cream

2 cups heavy cream

1 (14-ounce) can sweetened
  condensed milk

¾ teaspoon peppermint extract

2 or 3 drops green gel food coloring
  (optional)

1 cup mini chocolate chips

For the topping

2½ cups crushed mint Oreo
  cookies, divided

To make the no-churn ice cream

1. Line two 8-inch round cake pans with plastic wrap and set aside.

2. Whip the heavy cream in a stand mixer on medium-high speed until it forms stiff peaks.

3. Pour in the sweetened condensed milk, peppermint extract, and green food coloring (if using) and mix on medium-high until the mixture is thick.

4. Fold in the chocolate chips. Divide the ice cream mixture evenly between the two pans. Cover with plastic wrap and freeze overnight.

To make the cake

1. Preheat oven to 350°F. Line the bottom of an 8-inch round pan with parchment paper and spray with cooking spray. Set aside.

2. Sift the dry ingredients into a medium bowl and set aside.

3. Mix the buttermilk, oil, egg, and peppermint extract in a stand mixer on medium until fully incorporated. Lower the speed to low and mix in the dry ingredients until incorporated. Carefully pour the hot water into the batter and mix until combined.

4. Remove the bowl from the mixer and use a rubber spatula to ensure the ingredients are incorporated.

5. Pour the batter into the prepared cake pan. Bake for 25 minutes, or until a toothpick inserted into the middle comes out clean. Let cool in the pan for 10 minutes before transferring to a wire rack to finish cooling completely.

To construct the cake

1. On a cake plate, place the chocolate mint cake upside down. Place one layer of the ice cream evenly over the cake.

2. Sprinkle ½ cup of crushed cookies evenly over the ice cream. Place the other layer of ice cream on top. Sprinkle with the remaining 2 cups of crushed cookies.

3. Place the cake in the freezer to set for 30 minutes before covering tightly with plastic wrap and freezing until ready to serve.

4. Store leftovers, tightly covered in plastic wrap, in the freezer for 3 to 5 days.

TIP: When making no-churn ice cream, be sure to not overmix the cream, or you'll get butter, which is not what we're going for here! Whip the cream until you can turn the whisk upside down and the whipped cream holds its shape.

EPIC CHOCOLATE CHIP COOKIE ICE CREAM CAKE

· ·

MAKES **8 slices** | PREP TIME: **30 minutes, plus overnight to chill and 30 minutes to freeze** | COOK TIME: **30 minutes**

This is my ultimate birthday cake. Out of all of the ice cream cakes I've made, this is the one I make myself for my birthday every year. A fudgy layer of brownie and chocolate chunk ice cream are sandwiched in between two giant, buttery chocolate chip cookies. I have been caught eating the leftovers of this cake late at night, straight from the freezer.

For the cookies

Nonstick cooking spray
1 cup unsalted butter, at room
   temperature
1 cup granulated sugar
1 cup packed light brown sugar
2 eggs, at room temperature
1 tablespoon vanilla extract
3 cups all-purpose flour
½ teaspoon salt
2 teaspoons cornstarch
1 teaspoon baking powder
1 teaspoon baking soda
1½ cups semi-sweet chocolate chips

For the no-churn ice cream

2 cups heavy cream
1 (14-ounce) can sweetened
   condensed milk
1½ teaspoons vanilla extract
1 cup chopped milk chocolate

For the brownie

Nonstick cooking spray
10 tablespoons unsalted butter
1⅓ cups white granulated sugar
¾ cup plus 2 tablespoons cocoa powder
Pinch of salt
1 teaspoon vanilla extract
1 teaspoon chocolate extract
2 eggs
½ cup all-purpose flour

To make the no-churn ice cream

1. Line an 8-inch round cake pan with plastic wrap and set aside.

2. Whip the heavy cream in a stand mixer on medium-high speed until it forms stiff peaks.

3. Pour in the sweetened condensed milk and vanilla extract and mix on medium-high until the mixture is thick.

4. Fold in the chopped chocolate. Pour the mixture into the prepared pan, cover with plastic wrap, and freeze overnight.

To make the cookies

1. Preheat the oven to 350°F. Line the bottom of two 8-inch round cake pans with parchment paper and spray the pans with cooking spray.

2. Cream the butter, sugar, and brown sugar in a stand mixer on medium-high. Add the eggs and vanilla extract and mix until light and fluffy.

3. Lower the speed to low and mix in the flour, salt, cornstarch, baking powder, and baking soda until just combined. Fold in the chocolate chips.

4. Divide the cookie dough equally and press into the prepared pans. Bake for 8 minutes, or until the center is semi-set. Let cool in the pans before transferring the cookies to a wire rack.

5. Store in an airtight container at room temperature for up to 5 days.

To make the brownie

1. Preheat oven to 325°F. Line an 8-inch round baking pan with aluminum foil and spray with cooking spray. Set aside.

2. In a microwave-safe bowl, add the butter, sugar, cocoa powder, and salt. Microwave in 30-second intervals, stopping to stir after each interval, until the mixture is fairly smooth and hot to the touch, 1½ to 2½ minutes.

CONTINUED

3. Let cool for several minutes until the mixture is just warm to the touch. The mixture should look gritty. Using a wooden spoon, stir in the vanilla and chocolate extracts.

4. Add the eggs, one at a time, stirring vigorously after each one. Stir in the flour and beat the batter vigorously for 40 strokes. Spread the brownie batter into the prepared pan.

5. Bake for 22 to 25 minutes, or until a toothpick inserted into the middle comes out clean. Let cool in the pan completely.

6. Store in an airtight container at room temperature for up to 5 days.

To construct the cake

1. Place one chocolate chip cookie upside down on a plate.

2. Place the brownie on top and place the ice cream layer on the brownie. Top the ice cream with the second chocolate chip cookie.

3. Place the cake in the freezer to set for 30 minutes before covering tightly with plastic wrap and freezing until ready to serve.

4. Store leftovers, tightly covered with plastic wrap, in the freezer for 3 to 5 days.

TIP: If you want to make this cake party ready, drizzle fudge sundae sauce on top and add sprinkles.

GIANT ICE CREAM SANDWICH

MAKES 15 slices | PREP TIME: 20 minutes, plus 6 hours to chill and 30 minutes plus overnight to freeze | COOK TIME: 30 minutes

Ice cream sandwiches were always a staple in our freezer growing up. This would be a fun cake to serve at a party because it'll feed a crowd, and giant versions of food are always fun. You will need a large cake board to hold this crowd-pleasing ice cream cake.

For the cake

Nonstick cooking spray

3 eggs, at room temperature

1½ cups plus 1 tablespoon
    granulated sugar

2¼ cups all-purpose flour

¾ cup plus 1 tablespoon unsweetened
    dark cocoa powder

¾ teaspoon baking soda

½ teaspoon baking powder

½ teaspoon salt

1¼ cups mayonnaise

1 teaspoon vanilla extract

1⅓ cups hot, freshly brewed black coffee

For the ice cream

6 egg yolks

¾ cup granulated sugar

2 cups heavy cream, divided

1 cup whole milk

2 teaspoons vanilla bean paste

¼ teaspoon salt

½ cup store-bought caramel sauce

To make the ice cream

1. Place the bowl from the ice cream maker in the freezer overnight.

2. In a medium bowl, whisk together the egg yolks and sugar. In a medium pot over medium heat, scald 1 cup of heavy cream with the milk. Slowly whisk the milk-cream mixture into the egg mixture.

3. Transfer the mixture back to the pot and cook over medium heat, stirring constantly, until the custard is thick enough to coat the back of the spoon.

4. Pour the remaining 1 cup of cream into a large bowl. Pour custard mixture through a sieve or a fine-mesh strainer into the bowl with the cream and whisk to combine. Stir in the vanilla bean paste and salt.

5. Let the mixture cool to room temperature, 5 to 6 minutes. Transfer the bowl to the refrigerator and chill completely.

CONTINUED

6. Pour the chilled mixture into a 1½-quart ice cream maker and process the ice cream according to the manufacturer's directions. Five minutes before the ice cream is done, spoon in the caramel sauce.

7. Line a 9-by-13-inch baking pan with plastic wrap. Press the ice cream into the baking pan, place in the freezer, and let freeze completely.

To make the cake

1. Preheat the oven to 350°F and line two 9-by-13-inch baking pans with aluminum foil. Spray the pans with cooking spray. Set aside.

2. Combine the eggs and sugar in a stand mixer and mix on high until light and fluffy, 6 to 8 minutes.

3. In a medium bowl, whisk together the flour, cocoa powder, baking soda, baking powder, and salt. With the mixer on low, gently add the dry mixture to the sugar mixture, alternating with the mayonnaise. Add the vanilla extract and mix just until incorporated. Remove the bowl from the mixer and add the coffee, stirring by hand until combined. Use a rubber spatula to ensure the ingredients are incorporated.

4. Divide the batter evenly between the pans and bake for 15 to 18 minutes, or until a toothpick inserted into the middle comes out clean. Let cool in the pan for 10 minutes before transferring to a wire rack to finish cooling completely.

To construct the cake

1. Place one of the cakes upside down on a large cake board. Place the ice cream layer on top of the cake and top with the second cake, upside down.

2. Use the handle of a large wooden spoon or a straw to poke holes across the top of the cake to mimic an ice cream sandwich.

3. Place the cake in the freezer to set for 30 minutes before covering tightly with plastic wrap and freezing until ready to serve.

TIP: Mayonnaise is used in the cake recipe instead of oil or butter, which keeps the cake super moist and is a cheaper alternative to butter. Don't worry—you can't taste the mayonnaise. No one will ever guess the "secret ingredient."

ULTIMATE CANDY ICE CREAM CAKE

MAKES 8 to 10 slices | PREP TIME: 1 hour, plus overnight to chill and 30 minutes to freeze | COOK TIME: 24 minutes

This cake is inspired by my husband, whose diet can be described as "a ten-year-old who's been left unsupervised at a birthday party." Let's indulge along with him with this cake that's basically every kid's birthday cake dream. If you'd like to make this cake even more festive, add food coloring to the frosting.

For the cake

Nonstick cooking spray

1¾ cup all-purpose flour

1¾ cups granulated sugar

¾ cup unsweetened cocoa powder

2 teaspoons baking soda

1 teaspoon baking powder

¼ teaspoon ground nutmeg

Pinch of salt

1 cup buttermilk, at room temperature

½ cup canola oil

2 eggs, at room temperature

2 teaspoons vanilla extract

1 cup hot, freshly brewed black coffee

For the ice cream

2 cups whole milk

2 cups heavy cream

¾ cup granulated sugar

1 tablespoon vanilla extract or vanilla bean paste

¼ teaspoon salt

1½ cups M&M's

For the frosting

1½ cups unsalted butter, cut into pieces

5½ cups powdered sugar, divided

3 teaspoons vanilla extract

2 tablespoons heavy cream

½ teaspoon salt

Gel food coloring (optional)

For the candy

1 cup chopped Kit Kat bars

½ cup chopped Snickers bars

½ cup chopped Milky Way bars,

½ cup whole Rolo candies

¼ cup M&M's

CONTINUED

To make the ice cream

1. Place the bowl from the ice cream maker in the freezer overnight.

2. In a large bowl, whisk together the milk, cream, sugar, vanilla, and salt. Cover the bowl with plastic wrap and refrigerate the mixture overnight. Place the bowl from the ice cream maker in the freezer overnight.

3. Pour the chilled mixture into a 1½-quart ice cream maker and process according to the manufacturer's directions. Five minutes before the ice cream is done, add in the M&M's.

4. Line an 8-inch round cake pan with plastic wrap.

5. Pour the ice cream mixture into the prepared pan, wrap with plastic wrap, and freeze overnight.

To make the cake

1. Preheat the oven to 350°F. Line the bottom of two 8-inch round cake pans with parchment paper and spray with cooking spray. Set aside.

2. Sift the dry ingredients into a medium bowl and set aside.

3. Mix the buttermilk, oil, eggs, and vanilla extract in a stand mixer on medium speed, until combined. Lower the speed to low and mix in the dry ingredients until just incorporated. Slowly pour the hot coffee into the batter, mixing until combined.

4. Remove the bowl from the mixer and use a rubber spatula to ensure the ingredients are incorporated. Pour the batter into the prepared cake pan and bake for 24 minutes, or until a toothpick inserted into the middle comes out clean. Let cool in the pan for 10 minutes before transferring to a wire rack to finish cooling completely.

5. Store in an airtight container at room temperature for up to 3 days.

To make the frosting

1. Using the paddle attachment, whip the butter for 5 minutes in a stand mixer, until pale in color.

2. Pour in 2 cups of powdered sugar and mix on low until incorporated. Add 2 teaspoons of vanilla extract and mix until combined.

3. Add 2 more cups of powdered sugar and mix on low until incorporated. Increase the speed to medium-high and beat for 3 minutes. Add the remaining 1½ cups of powdered sugar, heavy cream, salt, and the remaining 1 teaspoon of vanilla extract. Add the food coloring (if using) and beat on low until incorporated. Increase the speed to medium-high and beat for another 5 minutes, or until smooth and fluffy.

To construct the cake

1. Place one layer of cake upside down on a cake plate. Using an offset spatula, spread half of the frosting over the cake. Scatter the Kit Kat pieces over the top.

2. Place the ice cream layer over the Kit Kat pieces and top with the second layer of cake, upside down. Spread the remaining frosting over the top and sides of the cake.

3. Sprinkle the Snickers pieces, Milky Way pieces, Rolos, and M&M's over the top.

4. Place the cake in the freezer to set for 30 minutes before covering tightly with plastic wrap and freezing until ready to serve.

5. Store leftovers in the freezer, tightly covered in plastic wrap, for 2 to 3 days.

TIP: Instead of the candies called for in the recipe, use your own favorites. Utilizing the bulk candy bins at the grocery store is a great way to get several types of candies in smaller amounts.

COOKIES AND CREAM ICE CREAM CAKE

MAKES 8 to 10 slices | PREP TIME: 45 minutes, plus overnight to chill and 30 minutes to freeze | COOK TIME: 35 minutes

Whoever thought of putting cookies in ice cream is a genius in my book. I added them to my no-churn ice cream, and it became one of my all-time favorites. Chocolate buttermilk cake is just a bit tangier than regular chocolate cake. The texture is light and airy, and it pairs well when frozen with ice cream.

For the cake

Nonstick cooking spray
¾ cup granulated sugar
¼ cup unsalted butter, at room temperature
1 egg, at room temperature
½ ounce unsweetened chocolate, melted
1 cup sifted cake flour
¼ teaspoon salt
⅛ teaspoon ground nutmeg
½ cup buttermilk, at room temperature
1 teaspoon vanilla extract
½ teaspoon baking soda
2 tablespoons white distilled vinegar

For the no-churn ice cream

2 cups heavy cream
1 (14-ounce) can sweetened condensed milk
1½ teaspoons vanilla extract
1½ cups chopped Oreo cookies

For the ganache

6 ounces white chocolate
1 ounce warm water

For the toppings

18 whole Oreo cookies
½ cup crushed Oreo cookies

To make the no-churn ice cream

1. Line an 8-inch square baking pan with plastic wrap. Set aside.

2. Whip the cream in a stand mixer on medium-high speed until it forms stiff peaks.

3. Add the sweetened condensed milk and vanilla extract and beat on medium-high until the mixture is thick. Fold in the Oreo chunks. Pour the ice cream mixture into the prepared pan, wrap with plastic wrap, and freeze overnight.

To make the cake

1. Preheat the oven to 350°F. Line the bottom of an 8-inch square pan with parchment paper and spray with cooking spray.

2. Mix the sugar and butter in the stand mixer on medium-high speed, until light and fluffy. Add the egg and the melted chocolate, and lower the speed to low. Mix together the flour, salt, and nutmeg in a small bowl. Add to the mixer in two batches, alternating with the buttermilk. Add the vanilla and mix until incorporated.

3. Remove the bowl from the mixer and use a rubber spatula to ensure the ingredients are incorporated.

4. In a small bowl, dissolve the baking soda in the vinegar and fold it into the batter. Pour the batter into the prepared cake pan and bake for 30 to 35 minutes, or until a toothpick inserted in the middle comes out clean. Let cool in the pan for 10 minutes before transferring to a wire rack to finish cooling completely.

To make the ganache

1. In a microwave-safe bowl, mix together the white chocolate and warm water.

2. Microwave in 30-second increments, stopping to stir in between, until the chocolate is melted. Let cool for 15 to 20 minutes before using.

To construct the cake

1. On a cake plate, place the buttermilk chocolate cake upside down.

2. Place the whole Oreo cookies in a single layer over the top. Place the ice cream layer over the cookies and spread with the white chocolate ganache. Sprinkle the crushed Oreos over the top.

3. Place the cake in the freezer to set for 30 minutes before covering tightly with plastic wrap and freezing until ready to serve.

4. Store leftovers in the freezer, tightly wrapped in plastic wrap, for 2 to 3 days.

TIP: When making the white chocolate ganache, keep an eye on that microwave like you would a two-year-old eating a chocolate bar on white carpet. Ganache can scorch easily.

WHITE CHOCOLATE CAKE

MAKES 8 to 10 slices | PREP TIME: 45 minutes, plus 6 hours to chill and
30 minutes plus overnight to freeze | COOK TIME: 45 minutes

This cake is rich in flavor and sure to impress—a layer of white chocolate cake with a thick and creamy custard-based butterscotch ice cream, and to top it all off, pieces of toffee for sprinkles. Butterscotch is my *favorite* ice cream topping, so if you happen to accidentally drizzle any on top of this cake, you won't hear any complaints from me!

For the cake

Nonstick cooking spray
1 (4-ounce) white chocolate baking
　bar, chopped
5 tablespoons unsalted butter, at room
　temperature
¾ cup granulated sugar
2 eggs, at room temperature
1 teaspoon vanilla extract
1 cup plus 2 tablespoons
　all-purpose flour
1⅛ teaspoons baking powder
⅛ teaspoon salt
⅛ teaspoon ground nutmeg
½ cup plus 2 tablespoons whole milk

For the ice cream

8 egg yolks
3½ tablespoons unsalted butter
1 cup packed dark brown sugar
2 cups heavy cream, divided
1½ cups whole milk
1 tablespoon vanilla extract
¼ teaspoon salt
1 cup toffee bits

For the toppings

2 cups toffee bits

To make the ice cream

1. Place the bowl from the ice cream maker in the freezer overnight.

2. In a medium bowl, beat the egg yolks. Set aside.

3. In a medium pot on medium heat, melt the butter. Stir in the brown sugar, bring to a simmer, and cook for 5 minutes. Pour in 1 cup of the cream and stir until smooth.

4. Remove from the heat and pour in the remaining 1 cup of cream, milk, vanilla extract, and salt. Return the pot to the heat and cook over medium heat, stirring occasionally, until you see steam rising. Slowly whisk ½ cup of the hot mixture into the egg yolks to temper them. Slowly add about half of the cream mixture to the eggs, stirring constantly. Pour the egg-cream mixture into the pot and continue to cook on medium heat, stirring constantly, until the custard is thick enough to coat the back of a spoon. Pour the mixture through a sieve into a large bowl or a storage container.

5. Cover the bowl with plastic wrap and refrigerate the mixture for at least 6 hours or overnight.

6. Pour the chilled mixture into a 1½-quart ice cream maker and process according to the manufacturer's directions. Fold in the toffee bits.

7. Line an 8-inch round cake pan with plastic wrap.

8. Pour the ice cream mixture into the prepared pan, cover with plastic wrap, and freeze overnight.

To make the cake

1. Preheat oven to 350°F and line the bottom of an 8-inch round cake pan with parchment paper. Spray the pan with cooking spray.

2. In a microwave-safe bowl, melt the chocolate in 15-second intervals, stirring in between. Set the chocolate aside to cool.

3. In a stand mixer, cream the butter and sugar on medium-high speed. Add the eggs, one at a time, mixing until light and fluffy. Mix in the vanilla.

4. Adjust the speed to low. Mix together the flour, salt, and nutmeg in a small bowl. Add to the mixer in two batches, alternating with the milk.

5. Remove the bowl from the mixer and use a rubber spatula to ensure the ingredients are incorporated.

6. Pour the batter into the prepared baking pan and bake for 28 to 30 minutes, or until a toothpick inserted in the middle comes out clean. Let cool in the pan for 10 minutes before transferring to a wire rack to finish cooling completely.

CONTINUED

To construct the cake

1. Place the cake upside down on a cake plate. Place the ice cream layer on top.

2. Gently press the toffee bits into the ice cream.

3. Place the cake in the freezer to set for 30 minutes before covering tightly with plastic wrap and freezing until ready to serve.

TIP: Investing in an oven thermometer can be helpful in making sure you're baking at the correct oven temperature, which results in more accurate baking times and a more even bake. To check if a cake is done, insert a toothpick into the middle of the cake. If the toothpick has raw batter on it, continue baking and check every 2 minutes until baked. If the toothpick comes out clean or with just a few crumbs on it, it's done.

CHOCOLATE WONDERLAND CAKE

. . . .

MAKES 8 to 10 slices | PREP TIME: 30 minutes, plus overnight to chill and 30 minutes to freeze | COOK TIME: 25 minutes

If you know me, then you know about my obsession with cereal, and Cocoa Krispies are one of my favorites. I coated them in chocolate here so they would stay nice and crispy. Layered with dark chocolate ice cream and a double chocolate cake, they make this a wonderland indeed.

For the cake

Nonstick cooking spray
1 cup semi-sweet chocolate chips
½ cup unsalted butter
¾ cup granulated sugar
2 teaspoons vanilla extract
Pinch salt
Pinch ground nutmeg
3 eggs, at room temperature
½ cup unsweetened cocoa powder
2 cups mini chocolate chips

For the no-churn ice cream

1 (14-ounce) can sweetened
   condensed milk
1 teaspoon vanilla extract
½ cup unsweetened dark cocoa powder
2 cups heavy cream

For the Cocoa Krispies

⅔ cup milk chocolate chips
1 tablespoon butter
2 cups Cocoa Krispies cereal

For the toppings

1 cup hot fudge sauce

To make the no-churn ice cream

1. Line a 9-inch springform pan with plastic wrap.

2. In a medium bowl, stir together the sweetened condensed milk, vanilla extract, and cocoa powder. Set aside.

3. Whip the heavy cream in a stand mixer on medium-high speed until it forms stiff peaks. Fold in the sweetened condensed milk mixture.

4. Pour the ice cream mixture into the prepared pan, cover with plastic wrap, and freeze overnight.

CONTINUED

To make the cake

1. Preheat the oven to 375°F. Line the bottom of a 9-inch springform pan with parchment paper. Spray the pan with cooking spray. Set aside.

2. In a large microwave-safe bowl, add the chocolate chips and butter. Melt in the microwave in 15-second intervals, stirring in between.

3. Stir in the sugar, vanilla, salt, and nutmeg. Add the eggs, one at a time, incorporating each egg completely before adding the next. Stir in the cocoa powder. Fold in the mini chocolate chips.

4. Pour the batter into the prepared pan and bake for 25 minutes. Let cool in the pan on a wire rack. Run a knife around the outside of the cake, loosening it from the sides of the pan. Release the springform pan and transfer the cake to a cake plate. Wrap the cake in plastic wrap and refrigerate.

To make the Cocoa Krispies

1. Have ready a sheet of aluminum foil.

2. In a microwave-safe bowl, heat the milk chocolate and butter in 15-second intervals, stirring in between, until completely melted. Stir the Cocoa Krispies into the melted chocolate mixture, coating the cereal completely.

3. Pour the coated cereal onto the foil in chunks, and let cool completely.

To construct the cake

1. Place the cake upside down on a cake plate. Spread 1 cup of the chocolate-covered Cocoa Krispies over the cake. Place the chocolate ice cream over the top.

2. In a microwave-safe bowl, heat the hot fudge sauce in the microwave for 10 seconds. Pour the hot fudge sauce over the top of the ice cream layer and top with the remaining chocolate-covered Cocoa Krispies.

3. Place the cake in the freezer to set for 30 minutes before covering tightly with plastic wrap and freezing until ready to serve.

TIP: If you only have one 9-inch springform pan, make the ice cream first, then freeze in tightly wrapped plastic wrap. Then use the springform pan to make the cake.

CHOCOLATE MALT MADNESS CAKE

MAKES 8 to 10 slices | PREP TIME: 35 minutes, plus overnight to chill and 30 minutes plus overnight to freeze | COOK TIME: 35 minutes

Whoppers are one of my favorite candies, and I *cannot* be trusted alone with a bag of them. There's something about that malt flavor combined with chocolate that's irresistible. Malt powder in the ice cream and cake lends a nutty, buttery flavor to this recipe. And of course, I had to top this cake with crushed Whoppers.

For the cake

Nonstick cooking spray

2 cups granulated sugar

1¾ cups all-purpose flour

¾ cup unsweetened cocoa powder

¼ cup malted milk powder

2 teaspoons baking powder

1½ teaspoons baking soda

½ teaspoon salt

⅛ teaspoon ground nutmeg

1 cup whole milk, at room temperature

½ cup canola oil

2 eggs, at room temperature

2 teaspoons vanilla extract

1 cup hot, freshly brewed black coffee

For the ice cream

⅓ cup unsweetened cocoa powder

¾ cup granulated sugar

6 tablespoons malted milk powder

2 cups heavy cream

1 cup whole milk

1 teaspoon vanilla extract

1 cup crushed Whoppers

For the ganache

½ cup heavy cream

1 cup semi-sweet chocolate chips

1 tablespoon butter

For the toppings

1 cup crushed Whoppers

To make the ice cream

1. Place the bowl from the ice cream maker in the freezer overnight.

2. In a large bowl, whisk together the cocoa powder, sugar, and milk powder. Slowly add the cream, milk, and vanilla extract and whisk until smooth. Cover the bowl with plastic wrap and refrigerate overnight.

CONTINUED

3. Pour the chilled mixture into a 1½-quart ice cream maker and process according to the manufacturer's instructions. Five minutes before the end of churning, add the crushed Whoppers.

4. Line an 8-inch round cake pan with plastic wrap.

5. Pour in the ice cream, cover the pan with plastic wrap, and freeze overnight.

To make the cake

1. Preheat oven to 350°F. Line the bottom of two 8-inch round cake pans with parchment paper. Spray the pans with cooking spray and set aside.

2. Mix the dry ingredients in a stand mixer until combined. Add the milk, oil, eggs, and vanilla and mix on medium until combined.

3. Adjust the speed to low and slowly pour in the hot coffee. Increase the speed to high and beat for 1 minute. Remove the bowl from the mixer and use a rubber spatula to ensure the ingredients are incorporated.

4. Evenly distribute the batter into the two prepared cake pans.

5. Bake for 30 to 35 minutes or until a toothpick inserted in the middle comes out clean. Let cool in the pans for 10 minutes before transferring to a wire rack to finish cooling completely.

To make the ganache

1. Pour the heavy cream and chocolate chips into a large microwave-safe bowl and add the butter.

2. Microwave in 30-second increments, stirring in between, until the chocolate is melted. Let cool for 15 to 20 minutes before using.

To construct the cake

1. Place one layer of chocolate cake upside down on a cake plate. Place the ice cream layer on the cake and top the ice cream with the second layer of chocolate cake.

2. Pour the cooled chocolate ganache over the cake and sprinkle with the crushed candies.

3. Place the cake in the freezer to set for 30 minutes before covering tightly with plastic wrap and freezing until ready to serve.

TIP: At the grocery store, malted milk powder can usually be found either next to the dried milk products in the baking aisle or next to the hot cocoa mixes.

CHOCOLATE-HAZELNUT ICE CREAM CUPCAKES

MAKES 12 cupcakes | PREP TIME: 20 minutes, plus overnight to freeze | COOK TIME: 17 minutes

This chocolate-hazelnut spread is life changing, let me tell you. Nutella is something I didn't have until I was an adult and now I'm making up for lost time. It pairs nicely with Crunch bars in the ice cream and makes the cupcakes really moist.

For the cupcake

1 cup all-purpose flour

½ teaspoon baking soda

¼ teaspoon baking powder

¼ teaspoon salt

⅛ teaspoon ground nutmeg

½ cup unsalted butter, at room temperature

1 cup granulated sugar

1 cup Nutella

2 eggs, at room temperature

1 teaspoon vanilla extract

6 tablespoons hot, freshly-brewed black coffee

6 tablespoons unsweetened cocoa powder

6 tablespoons heavy cream

For the no-churn ice cream

1 (14-ounce) can sweetened condensed milk

1 teaspoon vanilla extract

½ cup unsweetened cocoa powder

2 cups heavy cream

6 tablespoons Nutella

1 cup chopped Crunch bar

For the toppings

Chocolate sprinkles

To make the no-churn ice cream

1. Line a 9-by-5-inch loaf pan with plastic wrap.

2. In a medium bowl, whisk together sweetened condensed milk, vanilla extract, and cocoa powder. Set aside.

3. Whip the heavy cream in a stand mixer on medium-high speed until it forms stiff peaks.

4. Fold in the sweetened condensed milk mixture, Nutella, and Crunch bar pieces.

5. Pour the ice cream mixture into the prepared pan, cover with plastic wrap, and freeze overnight.

To make the cupcakes

1. Preheat the oven to 350°F and line a 12-cup cupcake tin with cupcake liners. Set aside.

2. In a small bowl, whisk together flour, baking soda, baking powder, salt, and nutmeg. Set aside.

3. In a stand mixer, cream together the butter, sugar, and Nutella on medium-high speed until light and fluffy. Add the eggs and mix until combined. Add the vanilla, coffee, and cocoa powder, adjust the speed to medium, and mix until combined.

4. Adjust the speed to low and add half of the flour mixture and half of the cream until incorporated. Repeat with the rest of the flour mixture and cream.

5. Remove the bowl from the mixer and use a rubber spatula to ensure the ingredients are incorporated.

6. Fill the cupcake liners ¾ full of batter and bake for 15 to 17 minutes, or until a toothpick inserted in the middle comes out clean. Transfer the cupcakes from the cupcake tin to a wire rack to cool.

7. Store the cooled cupcakes in an airtight container at room temperature.

To construct the cupcakes

When ready to serve the cupcakes, place 1 scoop of ice cream on top of each cupcake and top with chocolate sprinkles. These ice cream cupcakes are best eaten with a fork.

TIP: The ice cream cupcakes don't store well, so make them to order. And if you want to get a little crazy, remove the cupcake liner from the cupcake, place the cupcake in a bowl, microwave for 15 seconds, and then top with a scoop of ice cream and enjoy.

NEAPOLITAN
ICE CREAM SHAKE

MAKES **4 milkshakes** | PREP TIME: **20 minutes, plus overnight to freeze** | COOK TIME: **50 minutes**

Neapolitan is a combination of vanilla, chocolate, and strawberry. This shake, with chocolate ice cream, fresh strawberries, and vanilla pound cake for dipping, is the perfect blend of all three.

For the pound cake

Nonstick cooking spray

½ cup unsalted butter, at room temperature

⅔ cup granulated sugar

2 eggs, at room temperature

2 teaspoons vanilla extract

1½ cups all-purpose flour

1½ teaspoons baking powder

¼ teaspoon ground nutmeg

¼ teaspoon salt

½ cup heavy cream, at room temperature

For the no-churn ice cream

1 (14-ounce) can sweetened condensed milk

1 teaspoon vanilla extract

½ cup unsweetened cocoa powder

2 cups heavy cream

For the milkshake

2 cups chocolate ice cream

¼ cup whole milk

1 tablespoon hot fudge sauce

½ cup mini chocolate chips

1 cup quartered fresh strawberries

To make the no-churn ice cream

1. Line a 9-by-5-inch loaf pan with plastic wrap.

2. In a medium bowl, whisk together the sweetened condensed milk, vanilla extract, and cocoa powder. Set aside.

3. Whip the heavy cream in a stand mixer on medium-high speed until it forms stiff peaks. Fold in the sweetened condensed milk mixture.

4. Pour the ice cream mixture into the prepared pan, cover with plastic wrap, and freeze overnight.

To make the pound cake

1. Preheat the oven to 350°F. Line a 9-by-5-inch loaf pan with parchment paper and spray with cooking spray. Set aside.

2. In a stand mixer, beat the butter on medium-high until smooth and creamy. Add the sugar and beat until light and fluffy.

3. Add the eggs, one at a time, beating in the first completely before adding the next. Add the vanilla extract and beat until well incorporated.

4. In a small bowl, mix together the flour, baking powder, nutmeg, and salt. Adjust the speed to low and slowly mix half of the dry ingredients and ¼ cup of cream into the sugar mixture until barely combined. Add the remaining dry ingredients and the remaining ¼ cup of cream and mix until just combined.

5. Pour the batter into the prepared loaf pan and bake for 45 to 50 minutes, or until a toothpick inserted in the middle comes out clean. Let cool in the pan for 10 minutes before transferring to a wire rack to finish cooling completely.

Constructing the milkshakes

1. Cut the pound cake into 2-inch cubes and set aside.

2. Blend the ice cream, whole milk, and hot fudge sauce in a blender until it reaches your desired consistency. Fold in the chocolate chips by hand.

3. Divide the milkshake into 4 tall glasses and add a layer of strawberries. Serve with chunks of pound cake for dipping.

TIP: The chocolate no-churn ice cream is easy to make, but you can use leftover chocolate ice cream or store-bought ice cream instead. Add dollops of whipped cream and sprinkles to really complete this milkshake.

RED VELVET CELEBRATION PANCAKES WITH MAPLE-CREAM CHEESE ICE CREAM

MAKES 6 pancakes | PREP TIME: 20 minutes, plus overnight to chill and overnight to freeze | COOK TIME: 20 minutes

For the first five years at my job, I worked the night shift, and the only open places to eat late at night were Denny's or IHOP. So, my crew and I would eat "lunch" together at one or the other and I always ordered pancakes. This recipe is my tribute to those days.

For the pancakes

2 eggs, at room temperature

1¼ cups heavy cream (or milk of choice)

½ cup granulated sugar

2 tablespoons canola oil

1 teaspoon vanilla extract

1½ cups all-purpose flour

2 teaspoons unsweetened
  cocoa powder

1 tablespoon baking powder

¼ teaspoon salt

2 teaspoons red gel food coloring

Rainbow sprinkles

For the ice cream

8 ounces cream cheese, softened

1 cup whole milk

¾ cup sugar

1 tablespoon maple syrup

1 tablespoon maple extract

Pinch of salt

½ cup heavy cream

To make the ice cream

1. Place the bowl from the ice cream maker in the freezer overnight.

2. In a blender, add the cream cheese, milk, sugar, maple syrup, maple extract, and salt and blend until smooth.

3. Pour the mixture into a bowl and stir in the heavy cream. Cover the bowl with plastic wrap and refrigerate the mixture overnight.

4. Pour the chilled mixture into a 1½-quart ice cream maker and process according to the manufacturer's directions. Pour the ice cream into an air-tight container and freeze until ready to use.

To make the pancakes

1. In a large bowl, whisk the eggs together. Whisk in the cream, sugar, oil, and vanilla extract. Using a rubber spatula, stir in the dry ingredients and food coloring. Set the mixture aside for 5 minutes. (If the mixture gets too thick, stir in water 1 tablespoon at a time until you reach your desired consistency.)

2. Preheat a large nonstick skillet over medium heat. Pour 1 cup of pancake batter onto the skillet for each pancake and cook until bubbles form all across the top. Flip and continue cooking until each pancake is cooked through.

3. On individual plates, stack 2 pancakes on top of each other, top with a scoop of ice cream, and scatter with sprinkles. Serve immediately.

TIP: Ever wonder why your last pancake is fluffier than the first one you made? Setting the pancake batter aside for 5 minutes after making it allows the ingredients to marry and makes for a fluffier pancake. Now you know!

VANILLA ROLL CAKE

MAKES 12 slices | PREP TIME: 45 minutes, plus 2 hours to cool and
2 hours 30 minutes to freeze | COOK TIME: 7 minutes

Some call them cake rolls, and others call them roll cakes—either way, making them always intimidated me. Once I mastered the technique, I realized they weren't that hard and here I've included step-by-step directions to make it as easy as possible for you. I went classic here with the chocolate and vanilla flavors, but you could always sprinkle some candy or cookie pieces over the ice cream before rolling up the cake.

For the roll cake

2 egg whites

½ cup plus 1 tablespoon granulated
  sugar, divided

3 egg yolks

2 teaspoons vanilla extract

⅓ cup sifted cake flour

3 tablespoons cornstarch

¼ teaspoon salt

⅛ teaspoon ground nutmeg

Powdered sugar, for sprinkling

For the ice cream

1 cup unsweetened cocoa powder

⅔ cup granulated sugar

½ cup packed light brown sugar

1½ cups whole milk

3¼ cups heavy cream

2 tablespoons vanilla extract

To make the ice cream

1. Place the bowl from the ice cream maker in the freezer overnight.

2. In a large bowl, whisk together the cocoa powder, granulated sugar, and brown sugar. Whisk in the milk. Add the heavy cream and vanilla extract and whisk until smooth.

3. Cover the bowl with plastic wrap and refrigerate the mixture for 1 to 2 hours.

4. Pour the chilled mixture into a 1½-quart ice cream maker and process according to the manufacturer's directions. Pour the ice cream into an airtight container and freeze for at least 2 hours before using.

To make the roll cake

1. Preheat oven to 450°F and line a 17-by-12-inch jelly roll pan with parchment paper. Set aside.

2. Whisk the egg whites and 1 tablespoon of sugar in a stand mixer until stiff peaks form. Transfer the mixture into a small bowl and set aside.

3. Using the paddle attachment, mix together the egg yolks and remaining ½ cup of sugar on medium-high speed until pale and glossy. Mix in the vanilla extract.

4. Gently fold in the cake flour, cornstarch, salt, and nutmeg. Fold in the egg white mixture.

5. Spread the batter into the prepared baking pan in an even layer and bake for 6 to 7 minutes.

6. Have ready a clean tea towel. Remove the cake from the oven and sprinkle the top with powdered sugar. Invert the cake onto the tea towel and remove the parchment paper. Sprinkle with more powdered sugar and roll up the cake using the towel to help. Let the cake cool on a wire rack.

7. Remove the ice cream from the freezer 5 minutes before constructing the cake to allow it to soften some.

8. Unroll the cake and spread an even layer of ice cream over the entire cake. Roll the cake up again and place cake in the freezer for 30 minutes, before wrapping tightly in plastic wrap and freezing completely.

TIP: To make this recipe faster, use a high-quality store-bought ice cream, such as Breyers. And since the cake is vanilla flavored, just about any ice cream would work.

SPICY MEXICAN CHOCOLATE BUNDT ICE CREAM CAKE

· ·

MAKES **20 slices** | PREP TIME: **30 minutes, plus 2 hours to chill and 4 hours 30 minutes to freeze** | COOK TIME: **45 minutes**

For those who like their dessert with a little heat, the spice in this chocolate ice cream cake will hit you, but don't worry—it's just a hint, nothing that'll knock your socks off.

For the cake

Vegetable shortening

2¼ cups all-purpose flour, plus more for the pan, divided

1 cup warm water

⅔ cup unsweetened cocoa powder

¼ cup warm freshly brewed black coffee

¾ cup unsalted butter, at room temperature

1⅓ cups granulated sugar

⅓ cup packed light brown sugar

2 eggs, at room temperature

1½ teaspoons vanilla extract

4 teaspoons ground cinnamon

1¼ teaspoons baking soda

1 teaspoon cayenne pepper

¼ teaspoon baking powder

¼ teaspoon chili powder

¼ teaspoon salt

For the ice cream

1 cup unsweetened cocoa powder

⅔ cup granulated sugar

½ cup packed light brown sugar

1½ teaspoons cayenne pepper

1 teaspoon espresso powder

½ teaspoon chili powder

1½ cups whole milk

3¼ cups heavy cream

2 tablespoons vanilla extract

For the toppings

Chocolate ganache (optional, see page 75 for recipe)

Chocolate curls (optional)

To make the ice cream

1. Place the bowl from the ice cream maker in the freezer overnight.

2. In a large bowl, whisk together the cocoa powder, granulated sugar, brown sugar, cayenne pepper, espresso powder, and chili powder. Whisk in the milk until incorporated. Add the heavy cream and vanilla extract and mix together until smooth. Cover the bowl with plastic wrap and refrigerate the mixture for 1 to 2 hours.

3. Pour mixture into a 1½-quart ice cream machine and churn according to manufacturer's instructions. Remove the ice cream and freeze in an airtight container for at least 2 hours prior to using.

To make the cake

1. Preheat the oven to 350°F. Generously grease the inside of a 12-cup Bundt pan with vegetable shortening. Sprinkle flour over the shortening and tap out any excess.

2. In a small bowl, mix together the water, cocoa powder, and coffee. Set aside.

3. In a stand mixer, cream together the butter, granulated sugar, and brown sugar on medium-high speed until light and fluffy. Add the eggs, one at a time, incorporating the first egg completely before adding the next. Adjust the speed to low and mix in the cocoa powder mixture and vanilla extract. Add the flour, cinnamon, baking soda, cayenne, baking powder, chili powder, and salt and mix until barely incorporated.

4. Remove the bowl from the mixer and use a rubber spatula to ensure the ingredients are incorporated.

5. Pour the batter into the prepared Bundt pan and bake for 40 to 45 minutes, or until a toothpick inserted in the middle comes out clean. Let the cake cool in the pan for 30 minutes. Place a cake plate over the top of the pan, flip the pan, and release the cake onto the plate. Place the cake in the freezer for at least 1 hour to firm up before constructing the ice cream cake.

CONTINUED

To construct the cake

1. Let the cake sit at room temperature for 5 to 10 minutes to soften. Cut the cake in half, horizontally. Place the bottom half of the cake on a cake plate and spread an even layer of ice cream over the top of the cake. Place the top half of the cake on the ice cream.

2. Place the cake in the freezer to set for 30 minutes before covering tightly with plastic wrap and freezing for at least 1 hour or until ready to serve. Serve as is, or topped with chocolate ganache and chocolate curls.

TIP: I don't typically cook with vegetable shortening, but I keep it on hand for greasing Bundt pans. Dip a paper towel into the shortening and spread a thin layer of shortening in every crack, crevice, and detail of your Bundt pan. Sprinkle flour over the shortening, turn the Bundt pan on its side and gently tap it as you rotate the pan, to get an even sprinkle of flour. Tap out the excess flour. Properly preparing your Bundt pan makes all the difference and you'll be glad you did it when it's time to get the cake out of the pan.

CHAPTER THREE

Fruity

There is no time I look forward to more than when my favorite fruits come into season. I'm lucky to live in California where I have access to so many amazing fresh fruits. Strawberries are my favorite, and if I could make this entire chapter about strawberries, I probably would. But that would be boring, so you'll find a variety of fruit-flavored cakes and ice creams and combinations here. I made sure to use fruits that are readily available year-round, because when you want a fruit ice cream cake, you want it now, right?

FRUITY FLAKES ICE CREAM CAKE

MAKES 12 slices | PREP TIME: 45 minutes, plus 6 hours 30 minutes to freeze | COOK TIME: 17 minutes

Every week at the grocery store, my sister and I each got to pick out a box of cereal, and Fruity Pebbles was a favorite of mine that was *always* in my rotation. This cake is the tribute to all my childhood dreams.

For the cake

Nonstick cooking spray

1 cup unsalted butter, at room temperature

1¾ cups white granulated sugar

1 (3-ounce) box strawberry gelatin

4 eggs, at room temperature

1 tablespoon vanilla extract

1 teaspoon strawberry extract

1¾ cups all-purpose flour

1 cup cake flour

2½ teaspoons baking powder

¼ teaspoon salt

Pinch nutmeg

1 cup milk, at room temperature

1 cup chopped fresh strawberries

For the ice cream

¾ cup granulated sugar

1½ cups heavy cream

⅓ cup lime juice

2 tablespoons lime zest

2 teaspoons lime extract

For the clusters

1 cup vanilla almond bark or white candy melts

3½ cups Fruity Pebbles cereal

For the topping

1 (8-ounce) container whipped topping, thawed

To make the ice cream

1. Place the bowl from the ice cream maker in the freezer overnight.

2. In a large bowl, whisk together the sugar, cream, lime juice, lime zest, and lime extract, stirring until the sugar is dissolved. Cover the bowl with plastic wrap and refrigerate the mixture for 1 hour.

3. Pour the chilled mixture into a 1½-quart ice cream maker and process according to the manufacturer's directions.

CONTINUED

4. Line an 8-inch round cake pan with plastic wrap.

5. Pour in the ice cream, cover the pan with plastic wrap, and freeze for 4 to 6 hours before using.

To make the cake

1. Preheat the oven to 350°F. Line the bottom of two 8-inch round cake pans with parchment paper. Spray the pan with cooking spray.

2. Place the butter in a stand mixer and beat on medium-high speed until light and fluffy. Scrape down the sides of the bowl, add the sugar and strawberry gelatin, and mix until light and fluffy. Add the eggs, one at a time, fully incorporating each egg before adding the next. Beat in the vanilla extract and strawberry extract.

3. In a medium bowl, stir together the all-purpose flour, cake flour, baking powder, salt, and nutmeg. Add flour mixture and milk alternately and mix until combined. Fold in the strawberries.

4. Divide the batter evenly between the two prepared pans. Bake for 15 to 17 minutes, or until a toothpick inserted in the middle comes out clean.

5. Let cool in the pan for 10 minutes before transferring to a wire rack to finish cooling completely.

To make the clusters

1. In a microwave-safe bowl, melt the almond bark or white chocolate in 15-second intervals, stirring in between. Stir in the Fruity Pebbles, coating the cereal completely.

2. Place a sheet of aluminum foil on a work surface. Spread the Fruity Pebbles in a single layer on the foil. Let set for 1 to 2 hours.

To construct the cake

1. Place one layer of cake upside down on a cake plate. Spread half the whipped topping over the cake. Sprinkle 1 cup of Fruity Pebbles clusters over the whipped topping. Place the ice cream layer on top and place the second layer of cake on the ice cream.

2. Spread the remaining whipped topping on top and sprinkle the remaining Fruity Pebbles clusters over the top of the cake.

3. Place the cake in the freezer to set for 30 minutes before covering tightly with plastic wrap and freezing until ready to serve.

4. Store leftover cake in the freezer, tightly wrapped with plastic wrap, for 2 to 3 days.

TIP: Whipped topping, such as Cool Whip, comes frozen and needs to be thawed out before using. 1 to 2 days before constructing the cake, transfer the container of whipped topping from the freezer to the refrigerator to thaw and it will be ready to go.

PINEAPPLE UPSIDE-DOWN ICE CREAM CAKE

MAKES 12 slices | PREP TIME: 45 minutes, plus 4 hours to cool and
2 hours to freeze | COOK TIME: 1 hour

What happens when classic pineapple upside-down cake is sliced in half
and layered with a rich, brown sugar custard ice cream? You have a match
made in heaven.

For the ice cream

2 cups heavy cream

1 cup whole milk

⅔ cup packed light brown sugar

3 teaspoons ground cinnamon

¼ teaspoon ground nutmeg

¼ teaspoon salt

1½ teaspoons vanilla extract

5 egg yolks

For the glaze

Nonstick cooking spray

¼ cup unsalted butter

⅔ cup packed light brown sugar

½ teaspoon ground cinnamon

1 (20-ounce) can pineapple rings

For the cake

½ cup unsalted butter, at room
   temperature

¾ cup granulated sugar

¼ cup packed light brown sugar

2 eggs, at room temperature

2 tablespoons apple butter

1 teaspoon vanilla extract

½ teaspoon ground cinnamon

⅛ teaspoon ground nutmeg

1⅓ cups all-purpose flour

1 teaspoon baking powder

Pinch salt

¼ cup milk, at room temperature

To make the ice cream

1. Place the bowl from the ice cream maker in the freezer overnight.

2. In a medium pot over medium heat, heat the heavy cream, milk, brown sugar,
   cinnamon, nutmeg, and salt, whisking frequently, and bring to a simmer.
   Remove the pan from the heat and stir in the vanilla extract.

3. In a medium bowl, whisk together the egg yolks. Slowly whisk ½ cup of the hot cream mixture into the egg yolks to temper them. Pour in an additional ½ cup of the cream mixture, whisking constantly. Pour the egg mixture back into the pot, place back on the heat, and cook over medium heat until the mixture is thick enough to coat the back of a spoon.

4. Cover the bowl with plastic wrap and refrigerate the mixture for at least 4 hours or overnight.

5. Pour the chilled mixture into a 1½-quart ice cream maker and process according to the manufacturer's directions.

6. Line an 8-inch round cake pan with plastic wrap.

7. Pour in the ice cream, cover the pan with plastic wrap, and freeze for at least 2 hours before using.

To prepare the glaze

1. Line an 8-inch round cake pan with parchment paper. Spray the pan with cooking spray. Set aside.

2. In a small pot over medium heat, melt the butter. Stir in the brown sugar and let the mixture come to a boil, without stirring. Remove from the heat and stir in the cinnamon.

3. Pour the glaze evenly into the prepared pan. Gently place the pineapple rings evenly in a circle on top of the glaze. Set aside.

To make the cake

1. Preheat oven to 325°F.

2. In a stand mixer on medium-high, cream together the butter, granulated sugar, and brown sugar until light and fluffy, scraping down the sides of the bowl as needed.

3. Add the eggs, one at a time, mixing well after each addition. Add the apple butter, vanilla extract, cinnamon, and nutmeg and mix until creamy.

CONTINUED

4. Adjust the speed to low. Mix together the flour, baking powder, and salt in a small bowl. Add to the mixer in two batches, alternating with the milk until combined.

5. Remove the bowl from the mixer and use a rubber spatula to ensure the ingredients are incorporated.

6. Pour the batter into the pan and bake for 50 minutes or until a toothpick inserted in the middle comes out clean.

7. Let the cake cool on a wire rack for 10 minutes. Run a knife around the sides of the pan to loosen the cake. Place a plate on top of the cake pan, flip the pan over, and release the cake onto the plate. Let the cake cool completely on a wire rack. Cover the cake with plastic wrap and freeze 1 hour, or until firm.

To construct the cake

1. Freeze a cake plate for 1 hour prior to cake construction.

2. Place the ice cream layer on the plate and top with the cake. Serve immediately or wrap in plastic wrap and store in the freezer until serving.

3. This cake is best eaten within 3 to 5 days.

STRAWBERRY ICE CREAM SHORTCAKE

MAKES 15 slices | PREP TIME: 20 minutes, plus 1 hour 30 minutes and overnight to freeze | COOK TIME: 45 minutes

One of the best desserts my mom "made" for my sister and me growing up was sliced fresh strawberries, sprinkled with sugar and topped with milk. I would always try to sneak in a little more sugar when mom wasn't looking! We'd eat the strawberries first, then drink the strawberry-flavored milk. It was so good! The flavors in this cake remind me of that dessert.

For the cake

Nonstick cooking spray

2 cups finely chopped fresh strawberries

2 cups plus 1 tablespoon granulated sugar, divided

1½ cups all-purpose flour

1¼ teaspoons baking powder

¼ teaspoon salt

Pinch nutmeg

½ cup unsalted butter, at room temperature

1 egg, at room temperature

2 egg whites, at room temperature

1 tablespoon vanilla extract

¼ cup milk, at room temperature

For the no-churn ice cream

1 pound fresh strawberries, hulled

2 cups heavy cream

1 (14-ounce) can sweetened condensed milk

1 teaspoon strawberry extract

For the topping

1 (8-ounce) container whipped topping, thawed

1 (21-ounce) can strawberry pie filling

To make the no-churn ice cream

1. Line a 9-by-5-inch loaf pan with plastic wrap.

2. In a large bowl, mash the strawberries with a potato masher. Spread the mashed strawberries onto paper towels to soak up any excess juice.

CONTINUED

3.   Whip the heavy cream in a stand mixer on medium-high until thickens and forms stiff peaks. Fold in the sweetened condensed milk, strawberry extract, and mashed strawberries.

4.   Pour the ice cream into the prepared pan, cover with plastic wrap, and freeze overnight.

To make the cake

1.   Preheat the oven to 325°F. Line a 9-by-5-inch loaf pan with aluminum foil and spray with cooking spray. Set aside.

2.   In a medium bowl, mix together the strawberries and 1 tablespoon of sugar. Set aside.

3.   In another medium bowl, whisk together the flour, baking powder, salt, and nutmeg. Set aside.

4.   In a stand mixer, cream the butter on medium-high speed until light and fluffy. Scrape down the sides of the bowl as needed. Add the remaining 2 cups of sugar and mix until combined.

5.   Adjust the speed to low and add the egg, mixing completely. Add the egg whites and mix to combine. Add the vanilla extract and mix to combine.

6.   Add half of the flour mixture, mixing until just combined. Add the milk and mix until combined. Add the remaining flour mixture, mixing until just combined.

7.   Remove the bowl from the mixer and use a rubber spatula to ensure the ingredients are incorporated. Use a slotted spoon to add the strawberry mixture to the batter, leaving behind any excess liquid, and stir until just combined.

8.   Pour the batter into the prepared pan and bake for 40 to 45 minutes, or until a toothpick inserted in the middle comes out clean. Let cool in the pan for 10 minutes before transferring to a wire rack to finish cooling completely. Cover the cake in plastic wrap and freeze for 1 hour to firm up.

To construct the cake

1. Cut the cake in half, horizontally. Place the bottom half of the cake on a plate.

2. Cut the ice cream in half horizontally. Place one half of the ice cream on top of the bottom layer of cake. Add the second layer of cake and top with the remaining layer of ice cream.

3. Place the cake in the freezer to set for 30 minutes before covering tightly with plastic wrap and freezing for at least 1 hour or until ready to serve.

4. Top the cake with the whipped topping and strawberry pie filling and serve.

TIP: If a loaf cake starts to brown too quickly before the cake is fully baked, take a piece of aluminum foil and fold it in the shape of a tent. Place the foil loosely over the top of the cake and continue baking.

APPLE OF MY EYE
ICE CREAM CAKE

MAKES 20 slices | PREP TIME: 20 minutes, plus 2 hours 30 minutes and overnight to freeze | COOK TIME: 50 minutes

Apples, spice, and caramel are three flavors that definitely belong together. Easy, no-churn ice cream is loaded with apple pie filling and caramel sauce in this recipe, then layered with apple spice cake.

For the cake

Nonstick cooking spray

2½ cups all-purpose flour

2 teaspoons baking powder

1 teaspoon baking soda

2 teaspoons ground cinnamon

¾ teaspoon ground ginger

½ teaspoon ground nutmeg

¼ teaspoon ground cloves

¼ teaspoon ground mace

Pinch salt

1 cup canola oil

1¾ cups packed dark brown sugar

1 cup unsweetened applesauce, at room temperature

1 tablespoon molasses

4 eggs, room temperature

2 teaspoons vanilla extract

1 Granny Smith apple, peeled, cored, and grated or finely cut

For the no-churn ice cream

2 cups heavy cream

1 (14-ounce) can sweetened condensed milk

½ cup apple pie filling, cut into small chunks

½ cup caramel sauce

1 teaspoon vanilla extract

For the topping

1 (21-ounce) can apple pie filling

1 (8-ounce) container whipped topping, thawed

To make the no-churn ice cream

1. Line a 9-by-13-inch pan with plastic wrap.

2. Whip the heavy cream in a stand mixer on medium-high speed until it forms stiff peaks. Fold in in the sweetened condensed milk, apple pie filling, caramel, and vanilla extract.

3. Pour the mixture into the prepared pan, cover with plastic wrap, and freeze overnight.

To make the cake

1. Preheat the oven to 350°F. Line a 9-by-13-inch baking pan with parchment paper and spray with cooking spray. Set aside.

2. In a large bowl, whisk together the flour, baking powder, baking soda, cinnamon, ginger, nutmeg, cloves, mace, and salt.

3. In a stand mixer on medium speed, mix the canola oil, brown sugar, applesauce, and molasses until combined. Add the eggs, one a time, fully incorporating each one before adding the next. Add the vanilla extract and mix until combined.

4. Adjust the speed to low and add the flour mixture, mixing until combined. Remove the bowl from the mixer and fold in the apple. Pour the batter into the prepared baking pan.

5. Bake the cake for 45 to 50 minutes, or until a toothpick inserted in the middle comes out clean. If the cake starts to brown too much on top, cover with a folded piece of aluminum foil.

6. Let cool in the pan for 10 minutes before transferring to a wire rack to finish cooling completely. Cover the cake with plastic wrap and freeze for 1 hour to make it easier to cut.

To construct the cake

1. Cut the cake in half horizontally. Place the bottom half on a cake plate. Spread a layer of apple pie filling over the cake. Place the ice cream layer over the filling and top with the top half of the cake.

2. Use an offset spatula to frost the top and sides of the cake with whipped topping.

3. Place the cake in the freezer to set for 30 minutes before covering tightly with plastic wrap and freezing for at least 1 hour or until ready to serve.

TIP: To keep fresh apples from browning, sprinkle a little bit of lemon juice over them.

BANANA-RAMA PECANA ICE CREAM CAKE

MAKES 10 to 12 slices | PREP TIME: 30 minutes, plus overnight to chill and
4 hours to freeze | COOK TIME: 1 hour 10 minutes

Who doesn't love banana bread? It's probably one of the most requested
recipes people ask me to make. With butter pecan ice cream, this ice cream
cake is a fun twist on classic banana bread.

For the cake

Nonstick cooking spray

¼ cup unsalted butter, at room
  temperature

2 tablespoons canola oil

1 cup granulated sugar

5 tablespoons milk, at room
  temperature

½ tablespoon vanilla extract

2 eggs, at room temperature

2 large overripe bananas, mashed

2 cups all-purpose flour

1 tablespoon cinnamon

2 teaspoons baking powder

½ teaspoon baking soda

¼ teaspoon salt

⅛ teaspoon ground nutmeg

For the ice cream

1 cup whole milk

¾ cup packed light brown sugar

1 tablespoon butter

1 cup heavy cream

1 teaspoon vanilla extract

¼ to ½ cup pecan pieces

For the cinnamon-sugar mixture

5 tablespoons granulated sugar

2 tablespoons packed light brown sugar

½ teaspoon ground cinnamon

For the topping

¼ cup butterscotch sauce

¼ cup pecans

To make the ice cream

1. Place the bowl from the ice cream maker in the freezer overnight.

2. In a pot over low heat, mix together the milk, brown sugar, and butter just
   until the mixture starts to bubble around the edges. Remove from the heat
   and let cool completely. Stir in the heavy cream and vanilla extract.

3. Cover the bowl with plastic wrap and refrigerate the mixture overnight.

4. Pour the chilled mixture into a 1½-quart ice cream maker and process according to the manufacturer's directions. Five minutes before the churning is done, add the pecan pieces.

5. Line a 9-by-5-inch loaf pan with plastic wrap.

6. Pour in the ice cream, cover the pan with plastic wrap, and freeze for at least 4 hours or overnight.

To make the cinnamon-sugar mixture

In a small bowl, mix the granulated sugar, brown sugar, and cinnamon. Set aside.

To make the cake

1. Preheat the oven to 350°F. Line a 9-by-5-inch loaf pan with parchment paper and spray with cooking spray. Sprinkle 1 tablespoon of the cinnamon-sugar mixture into the pan. Set aside.

2. Beat the butter in a stand mixer on medium-high speed until creamy. Add the oil and beat until combined. Add the sugar and beat until fluffy, scraping down the sides of the bowl as needed.

3. Add the milk and vanilla extract and mix until combined. Add the eggs, one at a time, completely incorporating each egg before adding the next. Add the bananas and mix until combined.

4. Adjust the speed to low and slowly mix in the flour, cinnamon, baking powder, baking soda, salt, and nutmeg until just combined.

5. Remove the bowl from the mixer and use a rubber spatula to ensure the ingredients are incorporated.

6. Pour the batter into the pan and sprinkle the remaining cinnamon-sugar mixture on top, gently pressing it into the batter.

CONTINUED

7. Bake for 50 to 60 minutes, or until a toothpick inserted into the middle comes out clean.

8. Remove the loaf from the pan and let cool on a wire rack.

9. Store in an airtight container, at room temperature, for up to 3 days.

To construct the cake

1. Slice the cake in half horizontally. Place the ice cream layer on the bottom half of the cake and top with the other half of the cake.

2. Drizzle the butterscotch sauce over the top of the cake and sprinkle with pecans. Serve immediately, or place the cake in the freezer to set for 30 minutes before covering tightly with plastic wrap and freezing until ready to serve.

TIP: Kick this recipe up a notch by toasting the pecans first. In a small pot over medium heat, stir the pecans until they reach a warm brown color. Remove from the heat and let cool completely before adding to ice cream or topping the cake.

PINK LEMONADE
ICE CREAM CAKE

MAKES 8 to 10 slices | PREP TIME: 25 minutes, plus overnight to chill and overnight plus 1 hour 30 minutes to freeze | COOK TIME: 17 minutes

I prefer pink lemonade over regular lemonade, but I'm not sure if it's just because I prefer the flavor, or because I love the color pink so much. This cake is refreshing and would be a great treat to make for spring or summer get-togethers.

For the cake

Nonstick cooking spray

1 cup unsalted butter, at room temperature

1¾ cups granulated sugar

1 (3-ounce) box lemon gelatin

4 eggs, at room temperature

1 tablespoon vanilla extract

1 teaspoon lemon extract

1¾ cups all-purpose flour

1 cup cake flour

2½ teaspoons baking powder

¼ teaspoon salt

Pinch nutmeg

1 cup milk, at room temperature

1 tablespoon lemon zest

1 tablespoon lemon juice

For the ice cream

1½ cups heavy cream

1½ cups whole milk

1 cup granulated sugar

2 cups seedless raspberry jam

1 teaspoon vanilla extract

For the frosting

1½ cups unsalted butter, cut into pieces

5½ cups powdered sugar

1 tablespoon lemon extract

2 tablespoons heavy cream

1 tablespoon lemon zest

1 teaspoon vanilla extract

½ teaspoon salt

Pink gel food coloring (optional)

For the toppings

2 cups crushed lemon candies

CONTINUED

To make the ice cream

1. Place the bowl from the ice cream maker in the freezer overnight.

2. In a medium bowl, whisk together the cream, milk, and sugar. Whisk in the raspberry jam and vanilla extract.

3. Cover the bowl with plastic wrap and refrigerate the mixture overnight. Pour the chilled mixture into a 1½-quart ice cream maker and process according to the manufacturer's directions.

4. Line an 8-inch round cake pan with plastic wrap.

5. Pour in the ice cream, cover the pan with plastic wrap, and freeze overnight.

To make the cake

1. Preheat the oven to 350°F. Line the bottom of two 8-inch round cake pans with parchment paper. Spray the pan with cooking spray.

2. Beat the butter in a stand mixer on medium-high speed, until pale and glossy. Scrape down the sides of the bowl, add the sugar and lemon gelatin, and mix until light and fluffy. Add the eggs, one at a time, incorporating each egg fully before adding the next. Mix in the vanilla extract and lemon extract.

3. In a medium bowl, stir together the all-purpose flour, cake flour, baking powder, salt, and nutmeg.

4. Adjust the speed to low and add 1 cup of flour mixture to the batter in batches, alternating with the milk. Continue adding the flour mixture and milk and mix until combined. Fold in the lemon zest and lemon juice.

5. Remove the bowl from the mixer and use a rubber spatula to ensure the ingredients are incorporated.

6. Divide the batter evenly between the two prepared pans. Bake for 15 to 17 minutes, or until a toothpick inserted in the middle comes out clean. Let cool in the pan for 10 minutes before transferring to a wire rack to finish cooling completely.

To make the frosting

1. Whip the butter in a stand mixer on medium-high speed for 5 minutes, until pale in color. Adjust the speed to low and add 2 cups of powdered sugar until incorporated. Add the lemon extract and beat until combined. Add 2 more cups powdered sugar and beat on low until incorporated.

2. Adjust the speed to medium-high and beat for 3 minutes. Adjust the speed to low and add the remaining 1½ cups of powdered sugar, heavy cream, lemon zest, vanilla extract, and salt. Add the food coloring (if using). Beat until the ingredients are incorporated. Adjust the speed to medium-high and beat for another 5 minutes.

To construct the cake

1. Place one layer of lemon cake upside down on a cake plate and sprinkle 1 cup of the crushed lemon candies on top. Place the raspberry ice cream layer on the cake and top with the second layer of cake, upside down.

2. Frost the top and sides of the cake. Sprinkle the remaining crushed lemon candies on top.

3. Place the cake in the freezer to set for 30 minutes before covering tightly with plastic wrap and freezing for at least 1 hour, or until ready to serve.

4. This ice cream cake is best eaten within 3 days.

TIP: If you can only find jam with seeds in it, you can strain the jam through a fine-mesh strainer to remove the seeds before adding to the ice cream. And if you're opposed to using food coloring in the frosting, add a few tablespoons of the seedless jam to the buttercream frosting to get a pink hue.

ORANGE CREAMSICLE ICE CREAM CAKE

MAKES **8 slices** | PREP TIME: **20 minutes, plus overnight and 30 minutes to freeze** | COOK TIME: **17 minutes**

My hubby is all about a 50/50 bar, also called a Creamsicle. This cake has all the creamy orange flavors and will bring out the inner child in anyone.

For the cake

Nonstick cooking spray
1 cup unsalted butter, at room
    temperature
1¾ cups granulated sugar
1 (3-ounce) box orange gelatin
4 eggs, at room temperature
1 tablespoon vanilla extract
1 teaspoon orange extract
1¾ cups all-purpose flour
1 cup cake flour
2½ teaspoons baking powder
¼ teaspoon salt
Pinch nutmeg
1 cup milk, at room temperature
1 tablespoon orange juice
1 tablespoon orange zest

For the no-churn ice cream

2 cups heavy cream
1 (14-ounce) can sweetened
    condensed milk
1 teaspoon vanilla extract
1 teaspoon orange extract
½ tablespoon orange zest

For the toppings

1 teaspoon vanilla extract
1 (8-ounce) container whipped
    topping, thawed
1½ cups gummy orange slices

To make the no-churn ice cream

1. Line an 8-inch round pan with plastic wrap.

2. Whip the heavy cream in a stand mixer on medium-high speed until it forms stiff peaks. Fold in the sweetened condensed milk, vanilla and orange extracts, and orange zest.

3. Pour the ice cream mixture into the prepared pan, cover with plastic wrap, and freeze overnight.

To make the cake

1. Preheat the oven to 350°F. Line the bottom of two 8-inch round cake pans with parchment paper. Spray the pan with cooking spray.

2. Beat the butter in a stand mixer on medium-high speed until pale and glossy. Scrape down the sides of the bowl, add the sugar and orange gelatin, and mix until light and fluffy. Add the eggs, one at a time, incorporating each one fully before adding the next. Beat in the vanilla extract and orange extract.

3. In a medium bowl, stir together the all-purpose flour, cake flour, baking powder, salt, and nutmeg. Add 1 cup of flour mixture to the batter and alternate with the milk. Continue adding the flour mixture and milk and mix until combined. Fold in the orange juice and orange zest.

4. Remove the bowl from the mixer and use a rubber spatula to ensure the ingredients are incorporated.

5. Divide the batter equally between the two cake pans. Bake for 15 to 17 minutes, or until a toothpick inserted in the middle comes out clean.

6. Let cool in the pan for 10 minutes before transferring to a wire rack to finish cooling completely.

To construct the cake

1. Stir the vanilla extract into the container of whipped topping.

2. Place one layer of cake upside down on a cake plate. Spread half the whipped topping over the cake. Place the ice cream layer on top, and top with the remaining layer of cake.

3. Frost the cake with the remaining whipped topping and decorate with gummy orange slices.

4. Place the cake in the freezer to set for 30 minutes before covering tightly with plastic wrap and freezing until ready to serve.

5. Store any leftover cake in the freezer, tightly wrapped in plastic wrap, for 3 to 5 days.

TIP: When zesting citrus fruit, make sure you only get the skin and not the pith (the white part under the fruit skin), which can be bitter.

THE LIME IN THE COCONUT ICE CREAM CAKE

MAKES **20 slices** | PREP TIME: **30 minutes, plus overnight to chill and 1 hour 30 minutes to freeze** | COOK TIME: **2 hours**

I'm going tropical with this cake with lime and coconut, which always remind me of sunny vacations. When I need to get away but a trip to the Bahamas just isn't in the cards, I make this cake instead.

For the cake

Vegetable shortening

1½ cups unsalted butter, at room temperature

3 cups granulated sugar, plus more for the pan, divided

6 eggs, at room temperature

3 cups all-purpose flour

½ teaspoon baking powder

¼ teaspoon salt

⅛ teaspoon ground nutmeg

1 cup whole milk, at room temperature

1 teaspoon vanilla extract

1 teaspoon lime extract

3 teaspoons lime zest

⅓ cup lime juice

For the ice cream

2 cups heavy cream

1 (14-ounce) can coconut milk

1½ cups white granulated sugar

½ teaspoon vanilla extract

¼ teaspoon coconut extract

For the glaze

2 cups powdered sugar

3 tablespoons lime juice

2 tablespoons unsalted butter, melted

1 teaspoon vanilla extract

For the toppings

½ cup toasted sweetened coconut flakes

To make the ice cream

1. Place the bowl from the ice cream maker in the freezer overnight.

2. In a small pot over medium heat, stir together the cream, coconut milk, and sugar until it's just about to simmer. Lower the heat to low and cook, stirring occasionally, until the sugar dissolves, about 1 minute. Remove from the heat and stir in the vanilla and coconut extract.

3. Let the mixture cool in the pot for 20 minutes, transfer the mixture to a bowl, cover with plastic wrap, and refrigerate overnight.

4. Pour the chilled mixture into a 1½-quart ice cream maker and process according to the manufacturer's directions. Pour the mixture into an airtight container and freeze until ready to use.

To make the cake

1. Preheat the oven to 325°F. Grease and flour a 12-cup Bundt pan.

2. Cream the butter and sugar in a stand mixer on medium-high speed until light and fluffy. Add the eggs, one at a time, incorporating each one completely before adding the next.

3. In a small bowl, whisk together the flour, baking powder, salt, and nutmeg.

4. Adjust the speed to low, and add a small amount of the flour mixture and milk, alternating as you beat and ending with flour. Beat in the vanilla and lime extracts, lime zest, and lime juice.

5. Remove the bowl from the mixer and use a rubber spatula to ensure the ingredients are incorporated.

6. Pour the batter into the prepared Bundt pan and bake for 85 to 90 minutes, or until a toothpick inserted in the middle comes out clean.

7. Let the cake cool in the pan on a wire rack for 30 minutes before inverting onto a cake plate.

8. Store the cake in an airtight container, at room temperature.

To make the glaze

In a medium bowl, mix together the powdered sugar, lime juice, melted butter, and vanilla extract. If the mixture is too thick, add a small amount of water until desired consistency is reached. If mixture is too loose, add a small amount of powdered sugar until desired consistency is reached.

CONTINUED

To construct the cake

1. Remove the ice cream from the freezer 5 to 10 minutes before constructing cake to soften.

2. Cut the cake in half, horizontally, and place the bottom on a cake plate. Spread the ice cream over the cake in a thick layer. Add the top layer of cake and pour the glaze evenly over the top of the cake. Immediately sprinkle the toasted coconut flakes on top of the glaze.

3. Place the cake in the freezer to set for 30 minutes before covering tightly with plastic wrap and freezing for at least 1 hour, or until ready to serve.

TIP: There are many specialty extracts easily available now from the grocery store, at a craft or hobby store, or for purchase online. If you can't find one of the extracts in this recipe, you can omit them. Your cake will still taste amazing.

THE MONKEY IS CHUNKY ICE CREAM CAKE

MAKES **8 slices** | PREP TIME: **35 minutes, plus 4 hours to chill and overnight plus 1 hour 30 minutes to freeze** | COOK TIME: **25-30 minutes**

I got inspired from a certain duo's famous chocolate and banana ice cream and turned those flavors into an entire cake.

For the cake

Nonstick cooking spray

1 cup unsalted butter, at room temperature

2 cups granulated sugar

1 tablespoon vanilla extract

4 eggs, at room temperature

1 cup sour cream, at room temperature

½ cup heavy cream, at room temperature

3¼ cups cake flour

1½ teaspoons baking powder

½ teaspoon baking soda

½ teaspoon salt

¼ teaspoon ground nutmeg

For the ice cream

1 cup whole milk

½ cup granulated sugar

¼ cup packed light brown sugar

2 cups heavy cream

5 tablespoons instant banana cream pudding mix

1 teaspoon vanilla extract

2 bananas, cut into small chunks

1 cup chopped toasted walnuts

½ cup semi-sweet chocolate chips

For the ganache

1 cup semisweet chocolate chips

½ cup heavy cream

1 tablespoon butter

For the toppings

½ cup toasted walnut pieces

½ cup chopped bananas

To make the ice cream

1. Place the bowl from the ice cream maker in the freezer overnight.

2. In a large bowl, whisk together the milk, granulated sugar, and brown sugar until sugars have dissolved. Stir in the cream, pudding mix, and vanilla.

3. Cover the bowl with plastic wrap and refrigerate the mixture for at least 4 hours or overnight.

CONTINUED

4. Pour the chilled mixture into a 1½-quart ice cream maker and process according to the manufacturer's directions. Three minutes before the churning is done, add the banana chunks.

5. Line an 8-inch round cake pan with plastic wrap.

6. Pour in ⅓ of the ice cream and sprinkle with ½ of the walnuts and chocolate chips. Add another ⅓ of the ice cream and sprinkle with the remaining walnuts and chocolate chips. Add the remaining ice cream and smooth out the surface. Cover the pan with plastic wrap and freeze overnight.

To make the cake

1. Preheat the oven to 350°F. Line the bottom two 8-inch round pans with parchment paper and spray the pans with cooking spray. Set aside.

2. In a stand mixer on medium-high speed, cream the butter, sugar, and vanilla extract until light and fluffy. Scrape down the sides of the bowl and add the eggs one at time, incorporating each egg completely before adding the next.

3. Adjust the speed to low and mix in the sour cream and heavy cream. Add the flour, baking powder, baking soda, salt, and nutmeg and mix until just incorporated.

4. Remove the bowl from the mixer and use a rubber spatula to ensure the ingredients are incorporated.

5. Divide the batter equally between the two pans and bake for 20 to 22 minutes, or until a toothpick inserted in the middle comes out clean.

6. Let cool in the pan for 10 minutes before transferring to a wire rack to finish cooling completely.

To make the ganache

In a microwave-safe bowl, add chocolate chips, pour heavy cream over them, and add the butter. Microwave in 30-second increments, stopping to stir in between, until the chocolate is melted. Let cool for 15 to 20 minutes before using.

To construct the cake

1. Place one layer of cake upside down on a plate. Add the ice cream and top with the other layer of cake.

2. Pour the cooled ganache over the top and immediately sprinkle with toasted walnuts and banana chips.

3. Place the cake in the freezer to set for 30 minutes before covering tightly with plastic wrap and freezing for at least 1 hour, or until ready to serve.

TIP: To keep the bananas from browning, add 1 tablespoon of lemon juice to the chopped bananas.

CHEER YOU UP CHERRY ICE CREAM CAKE

MAKES 8 slices | PREP TIME: 45 minutes, plus 6 hours to chill and overnight plus 1 hour 30 minutes to freeze | COOK TIME: 50 minutes

Maraschino cherries are not only fun to say, they're fun to eat (no pits). This ice cream cake is full of cherry flavor and is sure to cheer anyone up on a cloudy day.

For the cake

Nonstick cooking spray

½ cup unsalted butter, at room temperature

1½ cups granulated sugar

4 egg whites

2 teaspoons vanilla bean paste

¼ teaspoon almond extract

2 cups cake flour

2 teaspoons baking powder

½ teaspoon baking soda

¼ teaspoon salt

⅛ teaspoon ground nutmeg

1⅓ cups buttermilk, at room temperature

1 (10-ounce) jar maraschino cherries, drained and finely chopped, 2 tablespoons juice reserved

For the ice cream

1 (16-ounce) jar maraschino cherries, drained and finely chopped, 2 tablespoons juice reserved

1¼ cups heavy cream, divided

1 cup whole milk

⅔ cup granulated sugar

¼ teaspoon salt

1 teaspoon vanilla extract

½ teaspoon cherry extract

1 cup mini chocolate chips

For the glaze

2½ cups powdered sugar

⅓ cup unsweetened cocoa powder

2 tablespoons butter, melted

1 teaspoon vanilla extract

Pinch salt

For the topping

1 (21-ounce) can cherry pie filling

To make the ice cream

1. Place the bowl from the ice cream maker in the freezer overnight.

2. In a medium pot over medium heat, mix together the cherries, ¼ cup of cream, milk, sugar, and salt and cook until the mixture just begins to boil. Turn off the heat, cover the top directly with plastic wrap, and let sit for 30 minutes.

3. Transfer the mixture to a blender and purée. Stir in the reserved cherry juice, 1 cup of cream, vanilla extract, and cherry extract. Transfer the mixture to a bowl, cover with plastic wrap, and refrigerate the mixture for at least 6 hours or overnight.

4. Pour the chilled mixture into a 1½-quart ice cream maker and process according to the manufacturer's directions. Three minutes before the churning is done, add the mini chocolate chips.

5. Line an 8-inch round cake pan with plastic wrap.

6. Pour in the ice cream, cover the pan with plastic wrap, and freeze overnight.

To make the cake

1. Preheat the oven to 350°F. Line the bottom of two 8-inch round cake pans with parchment paper and spray the pans with cooking spray. Set aside.

2. In a stand mixer on medium-high speed, cream together the butter and sugar until light and fluffy. Add the egg whites one at a time, incorporating each one completely before adding the next. Mix in the vanilla bean paste and almond extract.

3. In a small bowl, whisk together the flour, baking powder, baking soda, salt, and nutmeg. In a separate bowl, stir together the buttermilk and the reserved cherry juice.

4. Add flour mixture to the stand mixer, alternating with the buttermilk mixture, and mix on low until just combined. Fold in the cherries.

5. Divide the cake batter equally into the two cake pans and bake for 30 to 35 minutes, or until a toothpick inserted in the middle comes out clean.

CONTINUED

6. Let cool in the pan for 10 minutes before transferring to a wire rack to finish cooling completely.

7. Store the cakes in an airtight container at room temperature.

To make the glaze

1. In a medium bowl, stir together the powdered sugar, cocoa powder, butter, vanilla extract, and salt.

2. Pour in water, 1 teaspoon at a time, to thin the glaze out or add more powdered sugar to thicken the glaze to desired consistency.

To construct the cake

1. Place one layer of cake upside down on a cake plate. Spread a thin layer of cherry pie filling on the cake and top with the ice cream layer.

2. Place the second layer of cake on top and pour the chocolate glaze over it. Spread the remaining cherry pie filling on top of the glaze.

3. Place the cake in the freezer to set for 30 minutes before covering tightly with plastic wrap and freezing for at least 1 hour, or until ready to serve.

4. The ice cream cake should be eaten within 3 to 5 days.

TIP: Mini chocolate chips are used in the ice cream to ensure there's a bit of chocolate in every bite of ice cream. If you don't have mini chocolate chips, you can chop up regular chocolate chips with a sharp knife to get shavings and small pieces.

AN APPLE A DAY ICE CREAM CAKE

MAKES 10 to 12 slices | PREP TIME: 45 minutes, plus overnight and 2 hours 30 minutes to freeze | COOK TIME: 1 hour 30 minutes

This brown sugar cake is one of my favorite loaf cake recipes, and when you add apple butter ice cream to the middle, you'll reach a whole new level of deliciousness.

For the cake

Nonstick cooking spray

¾ cup unsalted butter, at room temperature

1½ cups packed light brown sugar

3 eggs, at room temperature

1½ cups all-purpose flour

¼ teaspoon baking powder

Pinch salt

Pinch ground nutmeg

½ cup French vanilla coffee creamer

1 teaspoon vanilla extract

For the no-churn ice cream

2 cups heavy cream

1 (14-ounce) can sweetened condensed milk

1 cup apple butter

1 teaspoon vanilla extract

For the topping

¼ cup caramel sauce

1½ cups apple pie filling

To make the no-churn ice cream

1. Line a 9-by-5-inch loaf pan with plastic wrap.

2. Whip the cream in a stand mixer on medium-high speed until it forms stiff peaks. Fold in the sweetened condensed milk, apple butter, and vanilla extract.

3. Pour the ice cream mixture into the prepared pan, cover with plastic wrap, and freeze overnight.

CONTINUED

To make the cake

1. Preheat the oven to 325°F. Line a 9-by-5-inch loaf pan with aluminum foil and spray the pan with cooking spray. Set aside.

2. In a stand mixer on medium-high speed, cream the butter and sugar. Add the eggs, one at a time, mixing well after each one, until fully incorporated.

3. In a small bowl, stir together the flour, baking powder, salt, and nutmeg. Adjust the speed to low, add half the flour mixture to the stand mixer and, alternating with half the coffee creamer, mix until combined. Add the remaining flour mixture and coffee creamer, then add the vanilla extract and mix until combined.

4. Pour the batter into the prepared pan and bake for 75 to 90 minutes, or until a toothpick inserted in the middle comes out clean.

5. Let cool in the pan for 10 minutes before transferring to a wire rack to finish cooling completely.

To construct the cake

1. Cut the cake in half horizontally and place the bottom on a cake plate. Cut the ice cream layer in half, horizontally, and place one half on top of the cake. Add the second layer of cake and second layer of ice cream.

2. Drizzle the caramel sauce over the top of the cake and spread a layer of apple pie filling over the caramel.

3. Place the cake in the freezer to set for 30 minutes before covering tightly with plastic wrap and freezing for at least 2 hours, or for up to 5 days.

TIP: Apple butter has a rich apple taste and is made of apples, brown sugar, apple cider, spices, and lemon juice. Apple butter is usually located near where the jams and jellies are sold at the grocery store.

BETTER THAN PUMPKIN PIE ICE CREAM CUPCAKES

MAKES 12 cupcakes | PREP TIME: 20 minutes, plus overnight to freeze | COOK TIME: 18 minutes

Next time it's your turn to bring dessert for Thanksgiving, make these ice cream cupcakes instead of pie and impress your family and friends.

For the cupcakes

½ cup canola oil

⅔ cup plus ½ cup packed light brown sugar, divided

½ cup granulated sugar

2 eggs, at room temperature

1 cup pumpkin purée

1½ teaspoons vanilla extract

1 cup all-purpose flour

1 teaspoon baking powder

½ teaspoon baking soda

2 teaspoons pumpkin pie spice

¼ teaspoon cinnamon

¼ teaspoon nutmeg

¼ teaspoon salt

2 cups fine graham cracker crumbs

2 tablespoons melted butter

Whipped topping, thawed, or whipped cream

For the no-churn ice cream

2 cups heavy cream

1 (14-ounce) can sweetened condensed milk

1 tablespoon vanilla bean paste

To make the no-churn ice cream

1. Line a 9-by-5-inch loaf pan with plastic wrap.

2. Whip the cream in a stand mixer on medium-high speed until it forms stiff peaks. Fold in the sweetened condensed milk and vanilla bean paste.

3. Pour the ice cream mixture into the prepared pan, cover with plastic wrap, and freeze overnight.

CONTINUED

To make the cupcakes

1. Preheat the oven to 350°F. Line a 12-cup cupcake tin with 12 cupcake liners. Set aside.

2. In large bowl, stir together the oil, ⅔ cup of brown sugar, the granulated sugar, eggs, pumpkin, and vanilla extract until incorporated. Stir in the flour, baking powder, baking soda, pumpkin pie spice, cinnamon, nutmeg, and salt.

3. In a bowl, stir together the graham cracker crumbs, melted butter, and the remaining ½ cup of brown sugar. Spoon a heaping tablespoon of the graham cracker mixture into the bottom of each cupcake liner, gently pressing the mixture down.

4. Fill the cupcake liners ⅔ full of batter. Bake for 15 to 18 minutes, or until a toothpick inserted in the middle comes out clean.

5. Let cool in the pan for 10 minutes before transferring to a wire rack to finish cooling completely.

6. Place in an airtight container at room temperature until time to serve.

To construct the cupcakes

1. Using a large ice cream scoop, place a scoop of ice cream on top of each cupcake. Top with a dollop of whipped topping or whipped cream and serve with a fork.

2. Leftover cupcakes topped with ice cream can be individually wrapped with plastic wrap and frozen.

TIP: When buying canned pumpkin, make sure you're buying pure pumpkin and not pumpkin pie filling or pie mix. Pumpkin pie filling or pie mix have added sugar and other ingredients made to simply pour into a pie shell and bake, which isn't what we want in these cupcakes.

ROLLING WITH PINEAPPLE ICE CREAM CAKE

MAKES 10 slices | PREP TIME: 30 minutes, plus 6 hours to chill and overnight plus 1 hour 30 minutes to freeze | COOK TIME: 25 minutes

Canned pineapple is used in the ice cream, cake, and topping, so you can make this cake year-round no matter when pineapple is in season.

For the cake

Nonstick cooking spray

1½ cups cake flour

½ tablespoon baking powder

¼ teaspoon salt

⅛ teaspoon nutmeg

3 egg whites

⅓ cup heavy cream, at room temperature

¼ cup plus 2 tablespoons canned crushed pineapple with its juice

2 tablespoons canola oil

1 teaspoon vanilla extract

1 cup granulated sugar

½ cup unsalted butter, at room temperature

For the ice cream

1 (20-ounce) can pineapple chunks

1 cup granulated sugar

¼ cup water

¾ cup heavy cream

2 teaspoons lemon juice

For the toppings

1 (3.4-ounce) box instant vanilla pudding mix

2 cups heavy cream

1 (15.25 ounce) can crushed pineapple, drained

To make the ice cream

1. Place the bowl from the ice cream maker in the freezer overnight.

2. In a blender, purée the pineapple, sugar, and water until smooth.

3. Transfer the mixture to a bowl and stir in the heavy cream and lemon juice. Cover the bowl with plastic wrap and refrigerate the mixture for at least 6 hours or overnight.

4. Pour the chilled mixture into a 1½-quart ice cream maker and process according to the manufacturer's directions.

CONTINUED

5. Line an 8-inch round cake pan with plastic wrap.

6. Pour in the ice cream, cover the pan with plastic wrap, and freeze overnight.

To make the cake

1. Preheat the oven to 350°F. Line the bottom of two 8-inch round cake pans with parchment paper and spray the pans with cooking spray.

2. In a medium bowl, whisk together the flour, baking powder, salt, and nutmeg and set aside. In a separate bowl, whisk together the egg whites, heavy cream, pineapple and its juice, canola oil, and vanilla extract and set aside.

3. In a stand mixer on medium-high speed, cream together the sugar and butter until light and fluffy. Adjust the speed to low and add half the flour mixture and half the pineapple mixture and mix until incorporated. Add the remaining flour mixture and pineapple and mix until combined.

4. Remove the bowl from the mixer and use a rubber spatula to ensure the ingredients are incorporated.

5. Divide batter equally between the two pans. Bake for 20 to 25 minutes, or until a toothpick inserted in the middle comes out clean.

6. Let cool in the pans for 10 minutes before transferring to a wire rack to finish cooling completely.

7. Store the cakes in an airtight container at room temperature.

To make the topping

1. With the paddle attachment of your stand mixer, mix the pudding mix and heavy cream on medium-high until light and fluffy. Fold in the drained pineapple.

2. Transfer mixture to a bowl and place in the refrigerator until ready to use.

To construct the cake

1. On a cake plate, place one layer of the pineapple cake upside down. Add the layer of pineapple ice cream on top of the cake and top with the second layer of cake.

2. Spread an even layer of the pineapple cream topping on top.

3. Place the cake in the freezer to set for 30 minutes before covering tightly with plastic wrap and freezing for at least 1 hour or until ready to serve.

4. The cake is best eaten within 2 to 3 days.

YOU'RE A PEACH BUNDT ICE CREAM CAKE

MAKES 16 to 18 slices | PREP TIME: 30 minutes, plus 6 hours to chill and overnight plus 2 hours 30 minutes to freeze | COOK TIME: 1 hour

Vanilla and cinnamon are used to flavor the Philadelphia-style ice cream sandwiched between layers of peach cake.

For the cake

Vegetable shortening

2 cups chopped fresh peaches

3 cups all-purpose flour, plus more for the pan, divided

1 cup unsalted butter, at room temperature

1½ cups granulated sugar

½ cup packed light brown sugar

4 eggs, at room temperature

2 teaspoons vanilla extract

1 teaspoon baking powder

1 teaspoon ground cinnamon

½ teaspoon salt

⅛ teaspoon ground nutmeg

For the ice cream

2 cups heavy cream

1 cup whole milk

⅔ cup granulated sugar

1 tablespoon molasses

1 tablespoon vanilla extract

1½ teaspoons ground cinnamon

¼ teaspoon salt

For the toppings

1 (21-ounce) can peach pie filling

To make the ice cream

1. Place the bowl from the ice cream maker in the freezer overnight.

2. In a large bowl, whisk together the cream, milk, sugar, molasses, vanilla extract, cinnamon, and salt. Cover the bowl with plastic wrap and refrigerate the mixture for at least 6 hours or overnight.

3. Pour the chilled mixture into a 1½-quart ice cream maker and process according to the manufacturer's directions.

4. Pour the ice cream into an airtight container and freeze overnight.

To make the cake

1. Preheat the oven to 325°F. Grease and flour a 10- to 12-cup Bundt pan. Set aside.

2. In a small bowl, mix the peaches with ¼ cup of flour. Set aside.

3. In a stand mixer on medium-high speed, cream together the butter, granulated sugar, and brown sugar until light and fluffy. Add the eggs, one at a time, mixing well after each one, and the vanilla extract. Adjust the speed to low and add the remaining 2¾ cups of flour, baking powder, cinnamon, salt, and nutmeg, mixing until just incorporated.

4. Remove the bowl from the mixer and use a rubber spatula to ensure the ingredients are incorporated. Fold in the peach-flour mixture and pour the batter into the prepared Bundt pan.

5. Bake for 50 to 60 minutes, or until a toothpick inserted in the middle comes out clean.

6. Let cool in the pan for 10 minutes. Place a plate on top of the pan and invert the pan to release the cake. Transfer the cake to a wire rack to finish cooling completely.

To construct the cake

1. Remove the ice cream from the freezer and let soften for 5 to 10 minutes.

2. Cut the cake in half, horizontally and place the bottom on a cake plate. Spread a 2- to 3-inch layer of ice cream over the cake. Spread half of the peach pie filling on top of the ice cream and top with the top half of the cake. Spread the remaining peach pie filling on top.

3. Place the cake in the freezer to set for 30 minutes before covering tightly with plastic wrap and freezing for 2 to 3 hours, or until ready to serve.

TIP: Using canned pie fillings is a quick and easy way to add flavor to desserts. You can also use homemade pie fillings, if you prefer to make them yourself.

DON'T BE BLUE
BLUEBERRY DONUT
ICE CREAM SANDWICHES

MAKES 15 to 17 donut sandwiches | PREP TIME: 25 minutes, plus overnight to chill and overnight to freeze | COOK TIME: 25 minutes

Donuts are all the craze right now, but frying donuts seems so messy to me. When I discovered donut baking pans, I was delighted. Baked donuts taste just like cake and these are sliced open and filled with a generous layer of blueberry ice cream. Maybe not appropriate for breakfast, but I won't judge.

For the donuts

Nonstick cooking spray

¼ cup unsalted butter, melted and cooled slightly

¼ cup canola oil

¾ cup granulated sugar

¼ cup packed light brown sugar

2 eggs, at room temperature

1½ teaspoons vanilla extract

¼ teaspoon ground cinnamon

¼ teaspoon ground nutmeg

2⅔ cups plus 1 tablespoon all-purpose flour, divided

1½ teaspoons baking powder

¼ teaspoon baking soda

¼ teaspoon salt

1 cup buttermilk, room temperature

1½ cups fresh blueberries

For the ice cream

1½ cups fresh blueberries

1¼ cups granulated sugar, divided

1 tablespoon lemon juice

1 cup whole milk

1 teaspoon vanilla extract

2 cups heavy cream

For the toppings

¼ cup melted butter

¼ cup granulated sugar

To make the ice cream

1. Place the bowl from the ice cream maker in the freezer overnight.

2. In a medium pot over medium heat, cook the blueberries, ½ cup of sugar, and lemon juice for 5 minutes. Transfer to a blender and purée until smooth. Pour the purée through a fine-mesh sieve or strainer to catch any seeds.

3. Return the purée to the pot and cook over medium heat, stirring constantly, for 15 minutes or until very thick. Transfer to a bowl, cover with plastic wrap, and refrigerate the mixture until cold.

4. In a bowl, whisk together the milk, remaining ¾ cup of sugar, and vanilla extract until the sugar has dissolved. Whisk in the chilled blueberry purée and heavy cream. Transfer mixture to a bowl, cover with plastic wrap, and refrigerate overnight.

5. Pour the chilled mixture into a 1½-quart ice cream maker and process according to the manufacturer's directions.

6. Line a 9-by-5-inch loaf pan with plastic wrap.

7. Pour in the ice cream, cover the pan with plastic wrap, and freeze overnight.

To make the donuts

1. Preheat the oven to 425°F. Spray two or three donut baking pans with cooking spray and set aside.

2. In a large bowl, stir together the butter, oil, granulated sugar, and brown sugar. Add the eggs one at a time, mixing well after each one. Add the vanilla extract, cinnamon, and nutmeg and mix until incorporated.

3. Add 1⅓ cups of flour, baking powder, baking soda, salt, and half of the buttermilk and mix until incorporated. Stir in the remaining 1⅓ cup of flour and remaining buttermilk and mix until combined.

CONTINUED

4. Toss the blueberries in a bowl with 1 tablespoon of flour. Fold the blueberries into the batter and transfer the batter into a large zipper-top bag. Snip off the corner of the bag and pipe the batter into the donut pan.

5. Bake, one pan at a time, for 8 to 9 minutes, until the donuts spring back when you press on them. Let donuts cool in the pan for 5 minutes before transferring them to a wire rack to finish cooling.

6. Store them in an airtight container at room temperature. They are best eaten within 2 to 3 days of baking.

To construct the donut sandwiches

1. Cut the donuts in half, horizontally. Cut the ice cream into 1-inch slices.

2. Place a slice of ice cream in the middle of each donut. Wrap each sandwich tightly with plastic wrap and freeze until ready to serve.

3. To serve, brush the top of each sandwich with melted butter and sprinkle with sugar.

TIP: If you only have one donut baking pan, let the pan cool completely before adding the donut batter for the next batch.

Strawberry Cheesecake Ice Cream Cupcakes 104

CHAPTER FOUR

Cheesecake

Ice cream cheesecakes may not be well known, but we're going to start a trend and make them the hot new thing. In this chapter, there are recipes for no-bake cheesecakes, cheesecake ice cream, cheesecake bars, and mini cheesecakes.

VERY VANILLA (BUT NOT ORDINARY) CHEESECAKE ICE CREAM BARS

MAKES 12 bars | **PREP TIME:** 30 minutes, plus 6 hours to chill and 24 hours to freeze (2 overnights) | **COOK TIME:** 2 minutes

These fun ice cream cheesecake bars are packed full of flavor and prove that vanilla does not mean boring! Each bar is a fun single-serving treat the whole family can enjoy.

For the crust

Nonstick cooking spray
6 tablespoons unsalted butter, melted
4 cups of finely crushed Nilla Wafers
½ cup powdered sugar
¼ teaspoon salt

For the ice cream

2 cups heavy cream
1 cup whole milk
⅔ cup granulated sugar
1 tablespoon vanilla bean paste
¼ teaspoon salt

For the cheesecake

2 cups white chocolate chips, finely chopped
1 cup heavy cream
8 ounces cream cheese, at room temperature
½ cup powdered sugar
1 tablespoon vanilla bean paste
½ teaspoon salt

To make the crust

1. Line a 9-inch square baking pan with aluminum foil and spray with cooking spray. Set aside.

2. In a bowl, mix together the butter, Nilla Wafer crumbs, powdered sugar, and salt.

3. Press the mixture firmly and evenly into the bottom of the pan. Place the pan in the freezer.

CONTINUED

To make the ice cream

1. Place the bowl from the ice cream maker in the freezer overnight.

2. In a large bowl, whisk together the cream, milk, sugar, vanilla bean paste, and salt. Place mixture in the refrigerator to chill overnight.

3. Cover the bowl with plastic wrap and refrigerate the mixture for at least 6 hours or overnight.

4. Pour half of the ice cream into the Nilla Wafer crust and freeze overnight. Pour the remaining half into an airtight container and freeze.

To make the cheesecake

1. In a microwave-safe bowl, melt the white chocolate chips in 15-second intervals, stopping to stir in between. Set aside to cool.

2. Whip the heavy cream in a stand mixer on medium-high speed until soft peaks form. Transfer to a bowl and set aside.

3. Using the stand mixer's paddle attachment, beat the cream cheese on medium-high speed until smooth and glossy. Scrape down the sides of the bowl, add the powdered sugar, melted white chocolate, vanilla bean paste, and salt and mix on medium-high until smooth and creamy. Add the whipped cream and mix until incorporated.

4. Spread the mixture on top of the ice cream in the 9-inch pan and freeze overnight.

To construct the bars

When ready to serve, cut into 12 squares. Store the leftovers in an airtight container and freeze. If you like, top with crushed Nilla Wafers or sprinkles.

TIP: Using room–temperature cream cheese is the key to a smooth and creamy cheesecake. To speed up the process of bringing cream cheese to room temperature, heat 1 cup of water in the microwave for 90 seconds. Remove the cup of water and place the cream cheese in the warm microwave and close the door. Check on the cream cheese periodically and remove once the cream cheese is soft.

CREAMY CHOCOLATE DREAMS CHEESECAKE

MAKES 8 slices | PREP TIME: 20 minutes, plus overnight to freeze | COOK TIME: 2 minutes

An Oreo cookie crust is topped with chocolate chip ice cream and a layer of chocolate cheesecake, making this the ultimate cookies and cream dessert.

For the crust

4 cups finely crushed Oreo cookies

6 tablespoons butter, melted

For the no-churn ice cream

2 cups heavy cream

1 (14-ounce) can sweetened condensed milk

2 teaspoons vanilla extract

1 cup semi-sweet chocolate chips

1 cup mini chocolate chips

For the cheesecake & toppings

1½ cups semi-sweet chocolate chips

11 ounces cream cheese, at room temperature

¾ cup powdered sugar

¼ cup unsalted butter, at room temperature

1 teaspoon vanilla extract

¼ teaspoon salt

2 cups whipped topping, thawed

2 cups Oreo cookie pieces

To make the crust

1. Line an 8-inch round cake pan with plastic wrap and set aside.

2. In a bowl, mix together the Oreo cookie crumbs and melted butter.

3. Press the mixture firmly and evenly into the bottom of the pan. Place the pan in the freezer.

To make the no-churn ice cream

1. Whip the heavy cream in a stand mixer on medium-high speed until it forms stiff peaks. Fold in the sweetened condensed milk, vanilla extract, semi-sweet chocolate chips, and mini chocolate chips.

2. Pour half of the mixture into the Oreo cookie crust and freeze overnight. Pour the remaining half into an airtight container and freeze.

CONTINUED

To make the cheesecake

1. Line an 8-inch round cake pan with plastic wrap.

2. In a microwave-safe bowl, melt the chocolate chips in 15-second intervals, stirring in between. Set aside to cool.

3. In a stand mixer on medium-high speed, beat the cream cheese until creamy. Adjust the speed to low, add the powdered sugar, butter, vanilla, and salt and beat until smooth. Slowly pour in the melted chocolate and mix until incorporated.

4. Fold in the whipped topping and pour the mixture into the prepared pan.

5. Cover the pan with plastic wrap and freeze overnight.

To construct the cake

1. Remove the ice cream and crust layer from the freezer. Remove the plastic wrap and place on a cake plate.

2. Place the cheesecake layer on the ice cream and top with crushed Oreo cookies. Serve immediately, or cover with plastic wrap and freeze.

TIP: There are many varieties of Oreo cookies available now, so use whatever flavor you fancy in this recipe.

CARAMEL APPLE ICE CREAM CHEESECAKE

MAKES 12 slices | PREP TIME: 1 hour, plus overnight and 2 hours to chill, and overnight and 1 hour to freeze | COOK TIME: 45 minutes

This is an ice cream cheesecake of epic proportions. Apple is the starring flavor in this cake, with caramel and spice playing supporting roles.

For the ice cream

2½ cups French vanilla coffee creamer

1 cup whole milk

1 cup white sugar

¼ cup packed light brown sugar

2 eggs, beaten

12 ounces cream cheese, cubed, at room temperature

2 teaspoons vanilla extract

2 teaspoons ground cinnamon

For the cheesecake

16 ounces cream cheese, at room temperature

½ cup granulated sugar

½ cup packed light brown sugar

1 teaspoon vanilla extract

¾ cup caramel sauce

1 teaspoon apple pie spice

4 ounces whipped topping, thawed

For the cake

Nonstick cooking spray

1 cup unsalted butter, at room temperature

2 cups granulated sugar

1 tablespoon vanilla extract

4 eggs, at room temperature

1 cup sour cream, at room temperature

½ cup heavy cream, at room temperature

3¼ cups cake flour

1½ teaspoons baking powder

½ teaspoon baking soda

½ teaspoon salt

2 tablespoons apple pie spice

For the crumble & toppings

2 cups fine graham cracker crumbs

3 tablespoons butter, melted

1 (21-ounce) can apple pie filling

To make the ice cream

1. Place the bowl from the ice cream maker in the freezer overnight.

2. Place a large bowl in the freezer. In a large pot over medium heat, cook the coffee creamer and milk until it reaches 175°F. Stir in the granulated sugar and brown sugar and cook until the sugars dissolve.

CONTINUED

3. In a small bowl, pour in the beaten eggs. Whisk ½ cup of the hot milk mixture into the eggs to temper them. Slowly whisk in another ½ cup of the hot mixture into the eggs.

4. Transfer the egg mixture to the pot and continue cooking on low heat until it coats the back of a spoon. Remove from the heat and whisk in the cream cheese until smooth. Stir in the vanilla extract and cinnamon.

5. Transfer the mixture to a bowl and cover with a piece of plastic wrap, pressing it directly on the mixture. Refrigerate overnight.

6. Line an 8-inch round cake pan with plastic wrap.

7. Pour the chilled mixture into a 1½-quart ice cream maker and process according to the manufacturer's directions.

8. Pour in the ice cream, cover the pan with plastic wrap, and freeze overnight.

To make the cheesecake

1. Line an 8-inch round cake pan with plastic wrap.

2. In a stand mixer on medium-high, beat the cream cheese until creamy. Add the granulated sugar, brown sugar, vanilla extract, caramel sauce, and apple pie spice and beat until fully incorporated.

3. Remove the bowl from the mixer and fold in the whipped topping. Pour the cheesecake into the prepared pan. Cover with plastic wrap and refrigerate for 1 to 2 hours before freezing overnight.

To make the cake

1. Preheat the oven to 350°F. Line the bottom of two 8-inch round pans with parchment paper and spray the pans with cooking spray. Set aside.

2. In a stand mixer on medium-high speed, beat the butter, sugar, and vanilla extract until light and fluffy. Scrape down the sides of the bowl and add the eggs, one at time, incorporating each one fully before adding the next.

3. Adjust the speed to low and mix in the sour cream and heavy cream. Add the flour, baking powder, baking soda, salt, and apple pie spice and mix until just incorporated.

4. Remove the bowl from the mixer and use a rubber scraper to ensure ingredients are fully incorporated.

5. Divide the batter equally between the two pans and bake for 20 to 22 minutes, or until a toothpick inserted in the middle comes out clean. Let cool in the pan for 10 minutes before transferring to a wire rack to finish cooling completely.

6. Store the cake in an airtight container at room temperature.

To make the crumble

1. Preheat the oven to 325°F. Line a cookie sheet with parchment paper.

2. In a small bowl, mix together the graham cracker crumbs and melted butter.

3. Spread the mixture onto a cookie sheet and bake for 10 minutes. Let cool and store in an airtight container for up to 3 days.

To construct the cake

1. Place one cake upside down on a cake plate. Spread a thin layer of apple pie filling on top and place the ice cream layer on top. Top with the second layer of cake.

2. Place the cheesecake on top of the cake. Spread a layer of apple pie filling on the cheesecake and sprinkle with the graham cracker crumble.

3. Place the cake into the freezer for at least 1 hour before serving. Wrap any leftover cake in plastic wrap and freeze for 3 to 5 days.

TIP: To make apple pie spice, mix ¼ cup ground cinnamon, 2 teaspoons ground nutmeg, 1 teaspoon ground ginger, and 1 teaspoon ground allspice. Store in a small jar in the pantry for up to 6 months.

STRAWBERRY CHEESECAKE ICE CREAM CUPCAKES

MAKES **24 cupcakes** | PREP TIME: **25 minutes, plus overnight to freeze** | COOK TIME: **22 minutes**

Instead of frosting, strawberry-flavored cupcakes are served with a scoop of graham cracker–cheesecake ice cream on top. You may never make classic cheesecake again.

For the cupcakes

2 cups finely chopped strawberries

2 cups plus 2 tablespoons granulated sugar, divided

3 cups all-purpose flour

2½ teaspoons baking powder

¼ teaspoon salt

Pinch nutmeg

1 cup unsalted butter, at room temperature

2 eggs, at room temperature

4 egg whites, at room temperature

1 tablespoon vanilla extract

½ cup whole milk, at room temperature

For the no-churn ice cream

2 cups heavy cream

8 ounces cream cheese, at room temperature

1 (14-ounce) can sweetened condensed milk

2 teaspoons vanilla extract

1½ cups crumbled graham crackers

For the toppings

Sprinkles (optional)

Strawberries, sliced (optional)

To make the no-churn ice cream

1. Whip the heavy cream in a stand mixer on medium-high speed until it forms stiff peaks. Transfer the cream to a bowl and set aside. Wipe the bowl clean and return to the stand mixer.

2. Using the paddle attachment, beat the cream cheese on medium-high speed until smooth and creamy. Scrape down the sides of the bowl, add the sweetened condensed milk and vanilla extract, and mix until smooth.

3. Fold in the whipped cream and graham cracker crumbles. Transfer to an airtight container and freeze overnight.

To make the cupcakes

1. Preheat the oven to 350°F. Line two 12-cup cupcake tins with cupcake liners. Set aside.

2. In a medium bowl, mix together the strawberries and 2 tablespoons of sugar. Set aside.

3. In a medium bowl, whisk the flour, baking powder, salt, and nutmeg. Set aside.

4. In a stand mixer on medium-high speed, beat the butter for 2 to 3 minutes, or until light and fluffy. Scrape down the sides of the bowl as needed. Add the remaining 2 cups of sugar and beat until combined.

5. Adjust the speed to low and add the eggs, one at a time, mixing well after each addition. Add the egg whites and mix until completely incorporated. Mix in the vanilla extract. Add half the flour mixture, mixing until just combined. Add the milk and mix until combined. Add the remaining flour mixture and mix until just combined.

6. Using a slotted spoon, add the strawberry mixture to the batter, leaving out any excess liquid, and stir until just combined.

7. Fill the cupcake liners ⅔ full of batter. Bake one tin at a time, for 20 to 22 minutes, or until a toothpick inserted in the middle comes out clean.

8. Let cool in the pan for 5 to 7 minutes before transferring to a wire rack to finish cooling completely.

To construct the cupcakes

Top each cupcake with a scoop of ice cream, add sprinkles or strawberries, and serve immediately. The ice cream cupcakes are best made to order.

COOKIES AND CREAM CHEESECAKE ICE CREAM CUPS

MAKES 12 to 14 ice cream cups | PREP TIME: 20 minutes, plus 2 hours to chill and overnight to freeze | COOK TIME: 50 minutes

As a young child, I refused to try cheesecake. I thought it had actual cheddar cheese in it and why would I want to eat that? Obviously, I now know that cheesecake got its name from *cream* cheese, not cheddar. It wasn't until my fifth grade teacher brought in mini cheesecake cups to share one day that I was brave enough to try it. It was love at first bite.

For the cupcakes

12 whole Oreo cookies
12 ounces cream cheese, at room temperature
½ cup granulated sugar
1 tablespoon unsweetened cocoa powder
1 tablespoon all-purpose flour
¼ cup sour cream, at room temperature
1 teaspoon vanilla extract
2 eggs, at room temperature
4 ounces milk chocolate chips, melted

For the no-churn ice cream

2 cups heavy cream
1 (14-ounce) can sweetened condensed milk
1 teaspoon vanilla extract
2 cups crushed Oreo cookies
½ cup mini chocolate chips

To make the no-churn ice cream

1. Whip the heavy cream in a stand mixer on medium-high speed until it forms stiff peaks.

2. Fold in the sweetened condensed milk, vanilla extract, crushed Oreo cookies, and chocolate chips.

3. Pour the ice cream into an airtight container and freeze overnight.

To make the cupcakes

1. Preheat the oven to 300°F. Line a 12-cup cupcake tin with 12 liners. Place a whole Oreo cookie on the bottom of each cupcake liner. Set aside.

2. In a stand mixer on low speed, beat the cream cheese, sugar, cocoa powder, and flour until just combined. Add the sour cream and vanilla extract and beat until combined. Add eggs, one at a time, mixing well after each.

3. Remove the bowl from the mixer and fold in the melted chocolate. Divide the mixture among the cupcake liners, filling almost to the top of each liner.

4. Bake for 15 minutes, turn the oven off, and leave the oven door closed for an additional 10 minutes. Crack the oven door open, and leave the cheesecakes in the oven for an additional 15 to 20 minutes.

5. Refrigerate the cheesecakes until completely cooled, at least 2 hours. Remove them from the cupcake tin, cover each one with plastic wrap, and refrigerate for up to 4 days.

To construct the ice cream cups

Top each cheesecake with a scoop of ice cream. Top with crushed Oreo cookies and serve immediately. They are best made to order.

TIP: If you need to construct all of your cheesecake ice cream cups ahead of time, you can do so, but wrap each cheesecake ice cream cup tightly with plastic wrap and store in the freezer until ready to serve. They should be eaten directly from the freezer within 2 days of construction.

Mimosas-for-All Ice Cream Cake 120

CHAPTER FIVE

Boozy

Who says ice cream cakes are just for kids? Not me! This chapter is all about booze. Alcohol adds a rich and robust flavor to ice cream cake, so I'm sharing the flavors of some of my favorite adult beverages in this chapter, from margaritas to Irish coffee. But don't worry, the alcohol in the cakes will burn off during baking, so three slices of cake won't leave you feeling like you need a Bloody Mary the next morning. Alcohol-infused frostings and uncooked ice cream bases that include alcohol will retain the most alcohol. Join me on this booze cruise and let's eat some cake.

BRINGING OUT THE RUSSIAN ICE CREAM CAKE

MAKES 10 slices | PREP TIME: 30 minutes, plus overnight to chill and overnight plus 1 hour 30 minutes to freeze | COOK TIME: 35 minutes

This cake is named after the White Russian cocktail: vodka, coffee liqueur, and cream over ice. My momma *loves* Kahlúa coffee liqueur, and when I was growing up, I remember watching her make drinks with it on the weekends. It always looked like dessert to me. I created this ice cream just for her.

For the cake

Nonstick cooking spray

2 eggs, at room temperature

1 cup plus 1 tablespoon granulated sugar

1½ cups all-purpose flour

½ cup plus 2 teaspoons cocoa powder

½ teaspoon baking powder

½ teaspoon baking soda

¼ teaspoon salt

⅔ cup plus 3 tablespoons mayonnaise, at room temperature

⅔ cup hot freshly brewed black coffee

¼ cup Kahlúa liquor

1 teaspoon vanilla extract

For the custard

4 egg yolks

½ cup granulated sugar

1 cup French vanilla coffee creamer

¼ teaspoon salt

1 cup heavy cream

1 teaspoon vanilla extract

For the buttercream frosting

1½ cups unsalted butter, cut into pieces

5½ cups powdered sugar

2 teaspoons vanilla extract

2 tablespoons heavy cream

1 tablespoon Kahlúa liquor

½ teaspoon salt

To make the custard

1. In a medium pot over medium heat, whisk together the egg yolks and sugar until the sugar dissolves. Remove from the heat.

2. In a small pot over medium heat, cook the coffee creamer and salt without stirring, just until it reaches a simmer. Return the egg mixture back to the heat and slowly whisk in the creamer, stirring constantly, until it reaches 165°F. Remove from the heat. Pour the mixture into an airtight container and chill in the refrigerator overnight. Place the ice cream freezer bowl in the freezer overnight.

CONTINUED

3. Stir the heavy cream and vanilla extract into the ice cream mixture.

4. Pour the chilled mixture into a 1½-quart ice cream maker and process according to the manufacturer's directions.

5. Line an 8-inch round cake pan with plastic wrap.

6. Pour in the ice cream, cover the pan with plastic wrap, and freeze overnight.

To make the cake

1. Preheat the oven to 350°F. Line the bottom of two 8-inch round cake pans with parchment paper and spray the pans with cooking spray. Set aside.

2. In a stand mixer on high speed, beat the egg and granulated sugar for 6 to 8 minutes. Scrape down the sides of the bowl.

3. In a medium bowl, whisk together the flour, cocoa powder, baking powder, baking soda, and salt.

4. Adjust the speed to low and add half the dry ingredients and the mayonnaise into the stand mixer, mixing until combined. Add the remaining flour mixture and mix until combined.

5. Remove the bowl from the mixer and stir in the coffee, Kahlúa, and vanilla extract. Divide the batter between the prepared pans. Bake for 13 to 15 minutes, or until a toothpick inserted into the middle comes out clean.

6. Let cool in the pan for 10 minutes before transferring to a wire rack to finish cooling completely.

To make the buttercream frosting

1. Whip the butter in a stand mixer for 5 minutes, until pale in color.

2. Adjust the speed to low, add 2 cups of powdered sugar, and mix until incorporated. Mix in the vanilla extract.

3. Add 2 more cups of powdered sugar and mix until incorporated. Adjust the speed to medium-high and beat for 3 minutes. Add the remaining powdered sugar, heavy cream, Kahlúa, and salt and beat on low until incorporated. Adjust the speed to medium-high and beat for another 5 minutes.

To construct the cake

1. Place one layer of cake upside down on a cake plate. Add the frozen vanilla custard layer and top with the second layer of cake. Frost the top and sides of the cake.

2. Place the cake in the freezer to set for 30 minutes before covering tightly with plastic wrap and freezing for at least 1 hour until ready to serve.

3. Store leftover cake tightly wrapped in plastic wrap, in the freezer, for up to 4 days.

TIP: If your custard base curdles, you can still save it. Let it cool to room temperature and purée it in a blender on medium-high speed for 30-seconds, or until smooth.

IRISH COFFEE EXTREME ICE CREAM CAKE

MAKES 12 slices | PREP TIME: 30 minutes, plus overnight and
1 hour 30 minutes for freezing | COOK TIME: 30 minutes

Irish coffee is for the coffee lover who wants to take it up a notch . . . with a little whiskey! This cake has layers of white chocolate mocha cake, Baileys ice cream, and whiskey-spiked buttercream.

For the cake

Nonstick cooking spray

6 ounces white chocolate

10 tablespoons unsalted butter, at room temperature

1¼ cups granulated sugar

2 eggs, at room temperature

1 cup French vanilla coffee creamer, at room temperature

1 teaspoon vanilla extract

3 cups all-purpose flour

1½ tablespoons baking powder

1 teaspoon espresso powder

For the no-churn ice cream

1 (14-ounce) can sweetened condensed milk

2 tablespoons light corn syrup

1 tablespoon Baileys Irish Cream

½ teaspoon vanilla extract

1¾ cups heavy cream

For the frosting

1½ cups unsalted butter, cut into pieces

5½ cups powdered sugar

2 teaspoons vanilla extract

2 tablespoons heavy cream

1 teaspoon whiskey

½ teaspoon salt

To make the no-churn ice cream

1. Line an 8-inch round cake pan with plastic wrap and set aside.

2. In a bowl, whisk together the sweetened condensed milk, corn syrup, Baileys, and vanilla extract. Set aside.

3. Whip the heavy cream in a stand mixer on medium-high speed until it forms stiff peaks. Add the sweetened condensed milk mixture and mix on medium until the mixture is thick.

4. Pour the ice cream into the prepared cake pan. Cover the pan with plastic wrap and freeze overnight.

To make the cake

1. Preheat the oven to 350°F. Line the bottom of two 8-inch round cake pans with parchment paper and spray the pans with cooking spray. Set aside.

2. In a microwave-safe bowl, melt the white chocolate in the microwave in 15-second intervals, stirring in between. Set aside to cool.

3. In a stand mixer on medium-high speed, cream the butter and sugar until light and fluffy.

4. Add the eggs, one at a time, mixing well after each one. Adjust the speed to low, add the coffee creamer, vanilla extract, flour, baking powder, and espresso powder, and mix until just combined. Add the melted chocolate and mix until incorporated.

5. Remove the bowl from the mixer and use a rubber spatula to ensure the ingredients are incorporated.

6. Divide the batter between the two prepared cake pans. Bake for 25 to 30 minutes, or until a toothpick inserted in the middle comes out clean. Let cool in the pan for 10 minutes before transferring to a wire rack to finish cooling completely.

7. Store in an airtight container at room temperature for up to 3 days.

To make the frosting

1. Whip the butter in a stand mixer on medium-high speed for 5 minutes, until pale in color.

2. Adjust the speed to low, add 2 cups of powdered sugar, and mix until incorporated. Add the vanilla extract and mix until combined.

3. Add 2 more cups of powdered sugar and mix until incorporated. Adjust the speed to medium-high and beat for 3 minutes.

4. Adjust the speed to low, add the remaining 1½ cups of powdered sugar, heavy cream, whiskey, and salt and beat until the ingredients are incorporated. Adjust the speed to medium-high and beat for another 5 minutes.

CONTINUED

To construct the cake

1. Place one layer of cake upside down on a cake plate. Add the ice cream layer and top with the second layer of cake. Frost the top and sides of the cake.

2. Place the cake in the freezer to set for 30 minutes before covering tightly with plastic wrap and freezing for at least 1 hour until ready to serve.

3. Store leftover ice cream cake, tightly wrapped in plastic wrap, in the freezer, for up to 4 days.

TIP: By adding alcohol to ice cream, it will make the ice cream softer. Adding corn syrup helps to stabilize it.

STOUT AND STRONG ICE CREAM CAKE

MAKES 12 slices | PREP TIME: 40 minutes, plus overnight and 1 hour 30 minutes for freezing | COOK TIME: 15 minutes

Guinness is probably the most commonly known stout, a dark beer that can be either dry or sweet. If you have never tried stout before, you may be surprised to know it's not the heavy, strong beer many think they are. Stouts have a touch of roastiness to them, with hints of chocolate and espresso, and they are actually low in alcohol content, which make them great to add to desserts.

For the cake

Nonstick cooking spray

2 eggs, at room temperature

1 cup granulated sugar

1½ cups all-purpose flour

½ cup plus 2 teaspoons cocoa powder

½ teaspoon baking powder

½ teaspoon baking soda

¼ teaspoon salt

⅔ cup mayonnaise

⅔ cup hot water

¼ cup stout-style beer

2 tablespoons hot fudge sauce

1 teaspoon vanilla extract

For the no-churn ice cream

¾ cup sweetened condensed milk

⅓ cup stout-style beer

1 tablespoon light corn syrup

1 teaspoon vanilla extract

1¼ cups heavy cream

1 cup mini chocolate chips

For the frosting

1¼ cups unsalted butter, at room temperature

3 cups powdered sugar

¾ cup unsweetened cocoa powder

½ tablespoon freshly brewed black coffee, at room temperature

½ tablespoon stout-style beer

5 tablespoons heavy cream

1 teaspoon vanilla extract

Pinch salt

CONTINUED

To make the no-churn ice cream

1. Line an 8-inch round cake pan with plastic wrap and set aside.

2. In a small bowl, stir together the sweetened condensed milk, stout, corn syrup, and vanilla extract. Set aside.

3. Whip the heavy cream in a stand mixer on medium-high speed until it forms stiff peaks. Add the sweetened condensed milk mixture and mix on medium until the mixture is thick.

4. Fold in the mini chocolate chips and pour the ice cream into the prepared pan. Cover with plastic wrap and freeze overnight.

To make the cake

1. Preheat the oven to 350°F. Line the bottom of two 8-inch round cake pans with parchment paper. Spray the pan with cooking spray. Set aside.

2. In a stand mixer on high speed, beat the egg and sugar for 6 to 8 minutes, until light and glossy. Scrape down the sides of the bowl.

3. In a medium bowl, whisk together the flour, cocoa powder, baking powder, baking soda, and salt.

4. Adjust the speed to low and add half the dry ingredients to the sugar mixture, mixing until just combined. Mix in the mayonnaise and then the remaining dry ingredients, until just combined.

5. Remove the bowl from the mixer and stir in the hot water, stout, hot fudge sauce, and vanilla extract until the batter is smooth. Divide the batter between the prepared pans.

6. Bake for 13 to 15 minutes, or until a toothpick inserted into the middle comes out clean. Let cool in the pan for 10 minutes before transferring to a wire rack to finish cooling completely.

To make the frosting

1. In a stand mixer on medium-high speed, beat the butter for 2 minutes. Adjust the speed to low and slowly add the powdered sugar and cocoa powder. Adjust the speed to medium and beat for about 2 minutes, until incorporated.

2. Adjust the speed to medium-low, add the brewed coffee, stout, heavy cream, vanilla extract, and salt and beat until incorporated. Adjust the speed to high and beat for 1 to 2 minutes. Add more powdered sugar or heavy cream to reach the desired consistency.

To construct the cake

1. Place one layer of cake upside down onto a cake plate. Add the ice cream layer and top with the second layer of cake.

2. Frost the top and sides of the cake.

3. Place the cake in the freezer to set for 30 minutes before covering tightly with plastic wrap and freezing for at least 1 hour until ready to serve.

4. Store leftover cake, tightly wrapped in plastic wrap, in the freezer for up to 4 days.

TIP: Pick a stout you enjoy drinking when buying the ingredients for this cake. Both dry and sweet stouts will work in the ice cream, cake, and frosting.

MIMOSAS-FOR-ALL ICE CREAM CAKE

MAKES 12 slices | PREP TIME: 30 minutes, plus overnight to chill and overnight plus 1 hour 30 minutes for freezing | COOK TIME: 27 minutes

My sister Wendy throws the *best* parties. She is known for her amazing mimosa bars that she sets up poolside with Champagne, fresh orange juice, and fresh fruit laid out for everyone to make their own drinks. This cake was inspired by her.

For the cake

2 cups Champagne

Nonstick cooking spray

2 cups granulated sugar

¾ cup unsalted butter, at room temperature

⅓ cup vanilla Greek yogurt, at room temperature

6 egg whites

1½ teaspoons vanilla extract

¾ cup heavy cream, at room temperature

2½ cups all-purpose flour

3½ teaspoons baking powder

¼ teaspoon salt

⅛ teaspoon ground nutmeg

For the sherbet

1 cup orange juice

¾ cup granulated sugar

2 tablespoons orange zest

1 tablespoon light corn syrup

2 cups whole milk

1 cup heavy cream

For the ganache

6 ounces white chocolate

1 ounce warm water

For the toppings

Oranges, sliced (optional)

Sprinkles (optional)

To make the sherbet

1. In a bowl, whisk together the orange juice, sugar, zest, and corn syrup until well combined. Whisk in the milk and heavy cream. Cover the bowl with plastic wrap and refrigerate overnight. Place the freezer bowl of an ice cream maker into the freezer overnight.

2. Pour the chilled mixture into a 1½-quart ice cream maker and process according to the manufacturer's directions.

3. Line two 8-inch round cake pans with plastic wrap.

4. Divide the sherbet between the two prepared pans, cover with plastic wrap, and freeze overnight.

To make the cake

1. In a pot over medium heat, bring the Champagne to a simmer and cook until the liquid reduces to 1 cup, about 10 minutes. Transfer the concentrated champagne to a small bowl and let cool to room temperature.

2. Preheat the oven to 350°F. Line the bottom of three 8-inch round cake pans with parchment paper. Spray the pans with cooking spray. Set aside.

3. In a stand mixer on medium-high speed, cream the sugar and butter until light and fluffy. Add the yogurt and mix until incorporated. Slowly add the egg whites and mix until incorporated. Scrape down the sides of the bowl and mix in the vanilla extract.

4. Adjust the speed to low and slowly pour in the heavy cream, reduced Champagne, flour, baking powder, salt, and nutmeg and mix until just combined.

5. Remove the bowl from the mixer and use a rubber spatula to ensure the ingredients are incorporated.

6. Divide the batter equally among the three prepared pans and bake for 22 to 25 minutes or until a toothpick inserted in the middle comes out clean. Let cool in the pan for 10 minutes before transferring to a wire rack to finish cooling completely.

7. Store the cakes in an airtight container at room temperature for up to 3 days.

To make the ganache

In a microwave-safe bowl, add the white chocolate and warm water. Microwave in 30-second increments, stirring in between, until the chocolate is melted. Let cool for 15 to 20 minutes before using.

CONTINUED

Construct the cake

1. Place one layer of cake upside down on a cake plate. Place one layer of sherbet on top. Add the second layer of cake, the second layer of sherbet, and the third layer of cake.

2. Pour the cooled ganache over the top of the cake.

3. Place the cake in the freezer to set for 30 minutes before covering tightly with plastic wrap and freezing for at least 1 hour until ready to serve.

TIP: Use your favorite type of Champagne for this recipe. Any dry Champagne, prosecco, or sparkling Moscato can be used. For a fun twist and a hint of color, try pink Champagne.

MARGARITA ICE CREAM CAKE

MAKES 20 slices | PREP TIME: 30 minutes, plus overnight to chill and overnight plus 1 hour 30 minutes for freezing | COOK TIME: 1 hour 40 minutes

This cake is all about the margarita. Lime ice cream is layered between a tequila-laced pound cake and doused in a lime-tequila glaze.

For the cake

Vegetable shortening

½ cup unsalted butter, at room temperature

½ cup canola oil

8 ounces cream cheese, at room temperature

3 cups granulated sugar

6 eggs, at room temperature

3 tablespoons lime juice

2 tablespoons lime zest

2 tablespoons tequila

1 teaspoon vanilla extract

3 cups all-purpose flour, plus more for the pan, divided

¼ teaspoon salt

⅛ teaspoon ground nutmeg

For the ice cream

1 (14-ounce) can sweetened condensed milk

1 cup whole milk

1 cup heavy cream

½ cup lime juice

¼ teaspoon salt

1 tablespoon lime zest

For the glaze

2 cups powdered sugar

2 tablespoons butter, melted

2 tablespoons lime juice

1 teaspoon tequila

To make the ice cream

1. In a medium bowl, whisk together the sweetened condensed milk, milk, heavy cream, lime juice, salt, and lime zest. Cover the bowl with plastic wrap and refrigerate the mixture overnight. Place the bowl from the ice cream maker in the freezer overnight.

2. Pour the chilled mixture into a 1½-quart ice cream maker and process according to the manufacturer's directions.

3. Pour the ice cream into an airtight container and freeze overnight.

CONTINUED

To make the cake

1. Preheat the oven to 325°F. Grease and flour a 10-cup Bundt pan. Set aside.

2. In a stand mixer on medium, beat the butter, oil, and cream cheese until combined. Add the sugar and mix until well combined.

3. Add the eggs one at a time, incorporating each egg completely before adding the next. Mix in the lime juice, lime zest, tequila, and vanilla extract. Adjust the speed to low, add the flour, salt, and nutmeg, and mix until barely combined.

4. Remove the bowl from the mixer and use a rubber spatula to ensure the ingredients are incorporated. Pour the batter into the prepared Bundt pan.

5. Bake for 1 hour 40 minutes, or until a toothpick inserted in the middle comes out clean.

6. Let cool in the pan for 10 minutes. Place a plate over the top of the pan, invert the pan, and release the cake from the pan. Let cool completely on a wire rack before storing in an airtight container at room temperature.

To make the glaze

In a medium bowl, mix together the powdered sugar, melted butter, lime juice, and tequila until combined. If the mixture is too thick, add hot water, 1 teaspoon at a time, until the desired consistency is reached. If the mixture is too thin, add powdered sugar until the desired consistency is reached.

To construct the cake

1. Cut the Bundt cake in half horizontally and place the bottom on a cake pan.

2. Spread 2 to 3 inches of ice cream over the cake. Top with the second half of the cake.

3. Pour the glaze over the top of the cake.

4. Place the cake in the freezer to set for 30 minutes before covering tightly with plastic wrap and freezing for at least 1 hour until ready to serve.

5. Store leftovers in the freezer, tightly wrapped in plastic wrap, for up to 3 days.

TIP: Sifting the powdered sugar will ensure a smooth glaze, free of clumps.

S'mores Amazingness Ice Cream Cake Bars 129

CHAPTER SIX

Artisanal

The cakes in this chapter embody the distinctive, hand-crafted nature of artisanal goods. Unique flavor combinations are featured in both the cake and ice cream and I have to say my inner Willy Wonka really came out as I created each recipe. They are whimsical, playful, and, most importantly, delicious.

S'MORES AMAZINGNESS
ICE CREAM CAKE BARS

. . . .

MAKES **12 bars** | PREP TIME: **40 minutes, plus overnight and
1 hour 30 minutes to freeze** | COOK TIME: **27 minutes**

I was a Girl Scout for several years, so if there's one thing I know, it's how
to make an awesome s'more. Now you can have s'mores anytime you want
with this ice cream cake. No campfire needed!

For the cake

Nonstick cooking spray

1 cup unsalted butter, at room
   temperature

½ cup granulated sugar

½ cup packed dark brown sugar

3 eggs, at room temperature

1 egg white

1¼ cups all-purpose flour

¾ cup fine graham cracker crumbs

1 teaspoon baking powder

½ teaspoon baking soda

½ teaspoon ground cinnamon

¼ teaspoon salt

⅛ teaspoon ground cloves

⅛ teaspoon ground nutmeg

½ cup buttermilk, at room temperature

½ cup vanilla Greek yogurt, at room
   temperature

1 tablespoon vanilla extract

For the no-churn ice cream

1 (14-ounce) can sweetened
   condensed milk

1 cup marshmallow crème

1 teaspoon vanilla extract

2 cups heavy cream

2 cups mini marshmallows

For the ganache

1 cup milk chocolate chips

½ cup heavy cream

1 tablespoon butter

For the topping

½ cup milk chocolate chips

¼ cup fine graham cracker crumbs

¼ cup mini marshmallows

To make the no-churn ice cream

1. Line an 8-inch square baking pan with plastic wrap and set aside.

2. In a small bowl, mix together the sweetened condensed milk, marshmallow
    crème, and vanilla extract.

CONTINUED

3. Whip the heavy cream in a stand mixer on medium-high speed until it forms stiff peaks. Pour in the sweetened condensed milk mixture and mix on medium-high until thick.

4. Fold in the marshmallows and pour the ice cream into the prepared pan. Cover the pan with plastic wrap and freeze overnight.

To make the cake

1. Preheat the oven to 350°F. Line the bottom of two 8-inch square baking pans with parchment paper and spray the pans with cooking spray. Set aside.

2. In a stand mixer on medium-high speed, cream the butter, granulated sugar, and brown sugar until light and fluffy. Add the eggs, one at a time, incorporating each one fully before adding the next. Mix in the egg white.

3. In a medium bowl, whisk together the flour, graham cracker crumbs, baking powder, baking soda, cinnamon, salt, cloves, and nutmeg. In a small bowl, whisk together the buttermilk, Greek yogurt, and vanilla extract.

4. Adjust the speed to low and add half the flour mixture and buttermilk mixture. Mix until just combined. Add the remaining flour mixture and buttermilk mixture and mix until just combined.

5. Remove the bowl from the mixer and use a rubber spatula to ensure the ingredients are incorporated.

6. Divide the batter equally between the two prepared baking pans and bake for 22 to 25 minutes, or until a toothpick inserted in the middle comes out clean. Let cool in the pan for 10 minutes before transferring to a wire rack to finish cooling completely.

7. Store the cakes in an airtight container, at room temperature for up to 3 days.

To make the ganache

1. In a microwave-safe bowl, add the chocolate chips and pour the heavy cream over them. Add the butter.

2. Microwave in 30-second increments, stirring in between, until the chocolate is melted. Let cool for 15 to 20 minutes before using.

To construct the cake

1. Place one layer of cake upside down on a cake plate. Add the ice cream layer and add the second layer of cake.

2. Pour the chocolate ganache on top and immediately sprinkle with the chocolate chips, graham cracker pieces, and mini marshmallows.

3. Place the cake in the freezer to set for 30 minutes before covering tightly with plastic wrap and freezing for at least 1 hour until ready to serve.

TIP: To achieve the fine graham cracker crumbs needed for this recipe, pulse graham crackers in a food processor until they become fine crumbs. If you don't have a food processor, place the graham crackers in a large zipper-top bag and smash with a rolling pin, flipping the bag over at least once during the process to ensure all the pieces become fine crumbs.

BUNNY'S FAVORITE ICE CREAM CAKE

MAKES **8 slices** | PREP TIME: **1 hour, plus overnight to chill and overnight plus 1 hour 30 minutes to freeze** | COOK TIME: **40 minutes**

Some bunny loves carrot cake and that would be my brother-in-law, Aaron. I'm the birthday cake baker in the family, so when his birthday rolls around I don't need to ask what he wants. I already know: carrot cake.

For the cake

Nonstick cooking spray

1 cup packed dark brown sugar

¾ cup canola oil

3 eggs, at room temperature

¼ cup sour cream, at room temperature

½ tablespoon vanilla extract

2 cups all-purpose flour

2½ teaspoons ground cinnamon

1½ teaspoons baking powder

½ teaspoon baking soda

½ teaspoon ground nutmeg

Pinch salt

2 cups finely grated carrots

For the ice cream

2½ cups heavy cream

1 cup whole milk

2 eggs, beaten

12 ounces cream cheese, cubed, at room temperature

1 tablespoon vanilla bean paste

½ teaspoon ground cinnamon

½ cup toasted pecan pieces

For the frosting

8 ounces cream cheese, at room temperature

½ cup unsalted butter, at room temperature

5 cups powdered sugar

1 tablespoon heavy cream

2 teaspoons vanilla extract

1 teaspoon ground cinnamon

¼ teaspoon salt

For the topping

1 cup toasted pecan pieces

To make the ice cream

1. Place a bowl in the refrigerator to chill while the ice cream is cooking.

2. In a large pot over medium heat, cook the cream and milk until it reaches 175°F.

3. Slowly whisk ¼ cup of the hot milk mixture into the bowl of eggs. Slowly whisk the egg mixture into the milk-cream mixture and continue to cook over low heat, whisking constantly, until the mixture reaches 160°F or it coats the back of a spoon.

4. Remove the pot from the heat, add the cream cheese, and stir until smooth. Pour the mixture into the chilled bowl and let cool for 2 minutes. Stir in the vanilla bean paste and ground cinnamon. Press a piece of plastic wrap directly onto the surface of the custard and refrigerate overnight. Place the ice cream maker bowl in the freezer overnight.

5. Pour the chilled mixture into a 1½-quart ice cream maker and process according to the manufacturer's directions. Five minutes before the churning ends, add the toasted pecans.

6. Line an 8-inch round cake pan with plastic wrap.

7. Pour in the ice cream, cover the pan with plastic wrap, and freeze overnight.

To make the cake

1. Preheat the oven to 350°F. Line the bottom of two 8-inch round cake pans with parchment paper and spray the pans with cooking spray. Set aside.

2. In a stand mixer on medium-high speed, beat the brown sugar and oil until combined. Add the eggs, one at a time, incorporating each one fully before adding the next. Add the sour cream and vanilla extract and beat thoroughly.

3. Adjust the speed to low, add the flour, cinnamon, baking powder, baking soda, nutmeg, and salt and mix until barely incorporated.

4. Remove the bowl from the mixer and fold in the carrots. Divide the batter equally between the prepared pans.

CONTINUED

5. Bake for 18 to 22 minutes, or until a toothpick inserted in the middle comes out clean. Let cool in the pan for 10 minutes before transferring to a wire rack to finish cooling completely.

6. Store the cakes, in an airtight container, at room temperature for up to 3 days.

To make the frosting

1. Beat the cream cheese in a stand mixer on medium-high until smooth and creamy. Add the butter and beat until creamy.

2. Adjust the speed to low and mix in the powdered sugar, heavy cream, vanilla extract, cinnamon, and salt. Adjust the speed to medium-high and beat for 3 minutes, until light and fluffy. You may need to add a little more heavy cream or powdered sugar to get your desired consistency.

To construct the cake

1. Place one layer of carrot cake upside down on a cake plate. Place the ice cream layer on the cake and top with the second layer of carrot cake.

2. Frost the top and sides of the cake and sprinkle with the toasted pecans.

3. Place the cake in the freezer to set for 30 minutes before covering tightly with plastic wrap and freezing for at least 1 hour until ready to serve.

4. Store any leftovers, tightly wrapped with plastic wrap, in the freezer for up to 5 days.

TIP: Use the finer side of a box grater to grate the carrots for the carrot cake. This ensures the carrot is well incorporated and baked in the cake.

CHURRO DELIGHT ICE CREAM CAKE

MAKES 8 slices | PREP TIME: 20 minutes, plus overnight and
1 hour 30 minutes to freeze | COOK TIME: 18 minutes

Is there anything better than a warm, freshly fried churro? That cinnamon-sugar coating, crunchy exterior, and soft center is so delicious. I thought it would be great in an ice cream cake, so I took those distinctive flavors and created this dessert by layering spice cake with vanilla-cinnamon ice cream and a vanilla-cinnamon glaze.

For the cake

Nonstick cooking spray

2¾ cups all-purpose flour

3 teaspoons baking powder

1½ teaspoons ground cinnamon

½ teaspoon ground nutmeg

2 teaspoons ground allspice

¼ teaspoon ground cloves

¼ teaspoon salt

½ cup shortening

¼ cup unsalted butter, at room
temperature

1⅔ cups granulated sugar

5 eggs, at room temperature

1 tablespoon vanilla extract

1¼ cups whole milk, at room
temperature

For the no-churn ice cream

2 cups heavy cream

1 (14-ounce) can sweetened
condensed milk

2 teaspoons vanilla extract

1 teaspoon ground cinnamon

For the topping

1 teaspoon ground cinnamon

1 (8-ounce) container whipped
topping, thawed

To make the no-churn ice cream

1. Line two 8-inch round cake pans with plastic wrap and set aside.

2. Whip the heavy cream in a stand mixer on medium-high speed until it forms stiff peaks.

CONTINUED

3. Add the sweetened condensed milk, vanilla extract, and cinnamon and mix on medium-high until thick.

4. Divide the ice cream between the two prepared pans and freeze overnight.

To make the cake

1. Preheat the oven to 350°F. Line the bottom of three 8-inch round cake pans with parchment paper and spray the pans with cooking spray. Set aside.

2. In a medium bowl, whisk together the flour, baking powder, cinnamon, nutmeg, allspice, cloves, and salt. Set aside.

3. In a stand mixer on medium speed, beat the shortening and butter until light and fluffy, about 1 minute. Add the sugar and beat until the mixture is light and fluffy. Add the eggs, one at a time, incorporating each one fully before adding the next. Add the vanilla extract and mix to combine. Scrape down the sides of the bowl.

4. Add half the flour mixture and the milk and beat until just incorporated. Add the remaining flour mixture and beat until just incorporated.

5. Remove the bowl from the mixer and use a rubber spatula to ensure the ingredients are incorporated.

6. Divide the batter equally among the prepared cake pans. Bake for 15 to 18 minutes, or until a toothpick inserted in the middle comes out clean. Let cool in the pan for 10 minutes before transferring to a wire rack to finish cooling completely.

7. Store the cakes in an airtight container, at room temperature, for up to 3 days.

To make the topping

Stir the cinnamon into the whipped topping.

To construct the cake

1. Place one layer of cake, upside down on a cake plate. Place one of the ice cream layers on top. Add the second layer of cake, the second layer of ice cream, and top it with the third layer of cake.

2. Spread the cinnamon-infused whipped topping on top of the cake.

3. Place the cake in the freezer to set for 30 minutes before covering tightly with plastic wrap and freezing for at least 1 hour until ready to serve.

4. Store leftover cake, tightly wrapped in plastic wrap, in the freezer for 4 to 5 days.

TIP: There are several topping options to spice up this churro cake. Buy frozen churros in the frozen food section at the grocery store, bake them, cut them in pieces, and place them on top of the finished cake. General Mills makes Cinnamon Toast Crunch Churros cereal that would also be a fun addition on top.

MOCHA MADNESS
ICE CREAM CAKE

. . . .

MAKES 8 slices | PREP TIME: 20 minutes, plus overnight to chill and overnight plus 1 hour 30 minutes to freeze | COOK TIME: 25 minutes

My son loves anything coffee flavored. When I asked Ethan what the cake of his dreams would be, this is what he came up with. A cake made of layers of coffee-chocolate cake, mocha ice cream, and chocolate ganache. Mom tested, kid approved.

For the cake

Nonstick cooking spray

1 egg, at room temperature

½ cup plus 1 teaspoon granulated sugar

¾ cup all-purpose flour

¼ cup unsweetened cocoa powder

2 teaspoons espresso powder

¼ teaspoon baking powder

¼ teaspoon baking soda

Pinch salt

⅓ cup mayonnaise

Scant ½ cup hot freshly brewed black coffee

2 tablespoons hot fudge sauce

½ teaspoon vanilla extract

For the ice cream

1 cup heavy cream

¾ cup whole milk

½ cup granulated sugar

¼ cup freshly brewed black coffee, chilled

2 tablespoons hot fudge sauce

1 tablespoon unsweetened cocoa powder

½ cup chopped chocolate-covered espresso beans

For the ganache

1 cup semi-sweet chocolate chips

½ cup heavy cream

1 tablespoon butter

1 teaspoon espresso powder

For the topping

½ cup chopped chocolate-covered espresso beans

To make the ice cream

1. In a medium bowl, whisk together the cream, milk, sugar, coffee, hot fudge sauce, and cocoa powder. Cover the bowl with plastic wrap and refrigerate overnight. Place the ice cream maker bowl in the freezer overnight.

2. Pour the chilled mixture into a 1½-quart ice cream maker and process according to the manufacturer's directions. Five minutes before the churning ends, add the chocolate-covered espresso beans.

3. Line an 8-inch round cake pan with plastic wrap.

4. Pour in the ice cream, cover the pan with plastic wrap, and freeze overnight.

To make the cake

1. Preheat the oven to 350°F. Line the bottom of an 8-inch round cake pan with parchment paper and spray with cooking spray. Set aside.

2. In a stand mixer on high, beat the egg and sugar for 6 to 8 minutes. Scrape down the sides of the bowl.

3. In a medium bowl, whisk together the flour, cocoa powder, espresso powder, baking powder, baking soda, and salt.

4. Adjust the sped to low and add half the flour mixture into the sugar mixture, alternating with the mayonnaise, continuing until the flour mixture and mayonnaise have been mixed until combined.

5. Remove the bowl from the mixer and stir in the coffee, hot fudge sauce, and vanilla extract until smooth.

6. Pour the batter into the prepared pan and bake for 13 to 15 minutes, or until a toothpick inserted into the middle comes out clean.

To make the ganache

1. In a microwave-safe bowl, add the chocolate chips and pour the heavy cream over them. Add the butter and espresso powder.

2. Microwave in 30-second increments, stirring in between, until the chocolate is melted. Let cool for 15 to 20 minutes before using.

CONTINUED

To construct the cake

1. Place the layer of cake upside down on a cake plate. Add the ice cream layer and pour the cooled chocolate ganache on top. Sprinkle the chopped espresso beans on top.

2. Place the cake in the freezer to set for 30 minutes before covering tightly with plastic wrap and freezing for 1 hour until ready to serve.

3. Store leftover cake wrapped tightly in plastic wrap, in the freezer for 2 to 3 days.

TIP: Espresso powder is an intensely dark and concentrated instant coffee. It can be found where instant coffee is sold at the grocery store.

PEANUT BUTTER DECADENCE ICE CREAM CAKE

MAKES 8 slices | PREP TIME: 30 minutes, plus overnight and 1 hour 30 minutes to freeze | COOK TIME: 30 minutes

This cake is rich, decadent, and *full* of peanut butter flavor. And because chocolate and peanut butter go hand in hand, there are copious amounts of peanut butter chocolate candies in this cake. My nieces, Abi and Gwen, are the loves of my life, and they always love anything "Auntie KK" makes. I know they'd both love this over-the-top cake.

For the no-churn ice cream

1 (14-ounce) can sweetened
  condensed milk
½ cup creamy peanut butter
2 teaspoons vanilla extract
2 cups heavy cream
½ cup chopped Butterfingers

For the cake

Nonstick cooking spray
1½ cups all-purpose flour
2 teaspoons baking powder
½ teaspoon baking soda
¼ teaspoon salt
¼ teaspoon ground nutmeg
1 cup packed light brown sugar
⅓ cup creamy peanut butter
⅓ cup canola oil
1½ teaspoons vanilla extract
2 eggs, at room temperature
1 cup buttermilk, at room temperature

For the icing

½ cup unsalted butter
½ cup unsweetened cocoa powder
6 tablespoons evaporated milk
3¾ cups powdered sugar
1½ teaspoons vanilla extract
⅛ teaspoon salt

For the topping

1 cup Butterfinger bits
½ cup chopped Butterfingers
¼ cup Reese's Pieces
½ cup chopped Reese's Peanut
  Butter Cups

CONTINUED

To make the no-churn ice cream

1. Line an 8-inch round cake pan with plastic wrap and set aside.

2. In a medium bowl, mix together the sweetened condensed milk, peanut butter, and vanilla extract. Set aside.

3. Whip the heavy cream in a stand mixer on medium-high speed until it forms stiff peaks.

4. Add the sweetened condensed milk mixture into the whipped cream on medium-high until thick. Add the Butterfinger pieces 5 minutes before the ice cream is done churning.

5. Pour the ice cream mixture into the prepared pan, cover with plastic wrap, and freeze overnight.

To make the cake

1. Preheat the oven to 350°F. Line the bottom of two 8-inch round cake pans with parchment paper and spray the pans with cooking spray. Set aside.

2. In a medium bowl, whisk together the flour, baking powder, baking soda, salt, and nutmeg.

3. In a stand mixer on medium-high speed, cream together the brown sugar, peanut butter, and oil. Mix in the vanilla extract. Add the eggs one at a time, mixing well after each.

4. Adjust the speed to low and add half the flour mixture along with the buttermilk and mix until just combined. Add the remaining flour mixture and mix until combined.

5. Remove the bowl from the mixer and use a rubber spatula to ensure the ingredients are incorporated.

6. Divide the batter equally between the prepared cake pans and bake for 18 to 20 minutes, or until a toothpick inserted in the middle comes out clean. Let cool in the pan for 10 minutes before transferring to a wire rack to finish cooling completely.

7. Store the cakes in an airtight container, at room temperature, for up to 3 days.

To make the icing

1. In a medium pot over medium heat, mix together the butter, cocoa powder, and evaporated milk and bring mixture to a boil, whisking occasionally.

2. Add the powdered sugar, vanilla extract, and salt and whisk continuously for 30 to 60 seconds or until completely smooth. Let the icing cool before using.

To construct the cake

1. Place one layer of cake upside down on a cake plate. Sprinkle the Butterfinger bits over the cake and place the ice cream layer on top. Place the second layer of cake on top. Spread the icing on the top and sides of the cake.

2. Sprinkle the chopped Butterfingers, Reese's Pieces, and chopped Reese's Peanut Butter Cups over the top.

3. Place the cake in the freezer to set for 30 minutes before covering tightly with plastic wrap and freezing for 1 hour until ready to serve.

4. Store leftovers, tightly wrapped in plastic wrap, in the freezer for 3 to 5 days.

TIP: If your cake is domed on top after baking, place the cooled cake on a cutting board and use a bread knife to cut the domed part off of the cake so it's level.

ROOTING FOR ROOT BEER BUNDT ICE CREAM CAKE

MAKES 20 slices | PREP TIME: 30 minutes, plus overnight to chill and overnight plus 1 hour 30 minutes to freeze | COOK TIME: 50 minutes

This cake is loaded with the flavor of root beer sandwiched between sweet cream ice cream—just like a root beer float. Taking a bite of this cake is like being transported back to my childhood.

For the cake

Vegetable shortening

1½ cups granulated sugar

½ cup canola oil

2 tablespoons molasses

2 eggs, at room temperature

2 teaspoons vanilla extract

½ teaspoon root beer extract

1¾ cups all-purpose flour, plus more for the pan, divided

1½ teaspoons baking powder

1½ teaspoons baking soda

¼ teaspoon salt

1¾ cups root beer, at room temperature

For the ice cream

½ cup granulated sugar

2 tablespoons cornstarch

2 cups heavy cream

1 cup coffee creamer

¼ cup light corn syrup

½ teaspoon vanilla extract

For the topping

1 (8-ounce) container whipped topping, thawed

To make the ice cream

1. In a medium pot, whisk together the sugar and cornstarch over medium heat. Add the heavy cream, coffee creamer, corn syrup, and vanilla extract and whisk constantly until it reaches a gentle boil for 30 seconds.

2. Pour the mixture through a fine-mesh strainer into a bowl, cover with plastic wrap, and refrigerate overnight. Place the ice cream maker bowl in the freezer overnight.

3. Pour the chilled mixture into a 1½-quart ice cream maker and process according to the manufacturer's directions.

4. Pour the ice cream into an airtight container and freeze overnight.

To make the cake

1. Preheat oven to 350°F. Grease and flour a 10-cup Bundt pan and set aside.

2. In a stand mixer on medium-high speed, beat the sugar, oil, and molasses until combined. Add the eggs, one at a time, mixing well after each one. Add the vanilla extract and root beer extract. Adjust the speed to low and mix in the flour, baking powder, baking soda, and salt. Slowly pour in the root beer and mix until just combined.

3. Remove the bowl from the mixer and use a rubber spatula to ensure the ingredients are incorporated.

4. Pour the batter into the prepared Bundt pan and bake for 35 to 40 minutes, or until a toothpick inserted in the middle comes out clean.

5. Let cool in the pan for 10 minutes. Place a plate over the top of the Bundt pan, invert the pan, and release the cake from the pan. Let cool completely before storing at room temperature in an airtight container.

Construct the cake

1. Cut the cake in half, horizontally and place the bottom on a cake plate. Spread 2 to 3 inches of ice cream over the cake and top with the second half of the cake.

2. Place the cake in the freezer to set for 30 minutes before covering tightly with plastic wrap and freezing for at least 1 hour. When ready to serve, add dollops of whipped topping on top.

3. Store leftover cake in an airtight container in the freezer for 4 to 5 days.

TIP: International Delight makes a Sweet Cream–flavored coffee creamer that would be perfect for the ice cream. If you can't find that, French Vanilla is another great option.

MAPLE-BACON DONUT ICE CREAM CAKE

MAKES **12 donuts** | PREP TIME: **30 minutes, plus overnight to chill and overnight to freeze** | COOK TIME: **40 minutes**

I think maple-bacon donuts are the best thing out there—maple glaze on top of fried doughy goodness and a sprinkling of bacon? Yum! I've upped the ante by sandwiching donuts with maple-bacon ice cream and I've sprinkled even *more* bacon over the top. You can thank me later.

For the donuts

Nonstick cooking spray

¾ cup granulated sugar

¼ cup packed light brown sugar

¼ cup unsalted butter, melted and cooled

¼ cup canola oil

2 eggs, at room temperature

1 teaspoon vanilla extract

2 cups all-purpose flour

1½ teaspoons baking powder

¼ teaspoon baking soda

¼ teaspoon ground cinnamon

¼ teaspoon ground nutmeg

Pinch salt

1 cup buttermilk, at room temperature

For the ice cream

½ pound thick-cut bacon

1 cup maple syrup, divided

¼ cup packed light brown sugar

2 cups heavy cream

⅔ cup whole milk

1 teaspoon vanilla extract

½ teaspoon salt

½ teaspoon maple extract

To make the ice cream

1. Preheat the oven to 400°F. Line a large rimmed sheet and with foil and place a wire rack on top.

2. Lay bacon strips flat on the wire rack and brush the tops with ⅓ cup of maple syrup.

3. Sprinkle the brown sugar on top and bake for 15 minutes, or until desired crispiness is reached. Let bacon cool completely in the pan before storing in an airtight container at room temperature.

4. In a medium pot, bring the remaining ⅔ cup maple syrup to a boil over medium heat. Lower the heat to low and simmer for 5 minutes, until the syrup thickens. Remove from the heat and whisk in the heavy cream, whole milk, vanilla extract, salt, and maple extract. Transfer the mixture to a bowl, cover with plastic wrap, and refrigerate overnight. Place the ice cream maker bowl in the freezer overnight.

5. Pour the chilled mixture into a 1½-quart ice cream maker and process according to the manufacturer's directions. While the ice cream is churning, cut up the maple bacon into bits and measure out ½ cup. Five minutes before the churning ends, add the ½ cup of bacon bits. Transfer the ice cream to an airtight container and freeze overnight.

To make the donuts

1. Preheat the oven to 425°F. Spray two donut pans generously with cooking spray. Set aside.

2. In a large bowl, whisk the granulated sugar, brown sugar, butter, and oil until incorporated. Add the eggs, one at a time, mixing well after each one. Mix in the vanilla extract.

3. In a small bowl combine the flour, baking powder, baking soda, cinnamon, nutmeg, and salt. Stir half of the flour mixture into the butter-sugar mixture and mix until combined. Add the buttermilk and mix thoroughly. Add the remaining flour mixture and mix until incorporated.

4. Pour the batter into a large zipper-top bag. Snip off a corner of the bag and pipe the batter into the donut pans, filling the cavities to the top.

5. Bake, one pan at a time, for 9 minutes. Transfer the donuts from the pan to a wire rack to cool.

6. Store the donuts in an airtight container at room temperature. Donuts are best eaten within 2 to 3 days.

CONTINUED

To construct the cake

1. Lay 5 donuts on a large platter in a circle, in the shape of a cake. Add 1 scoop of ice cream on top of each donut and sprinkle with additional candied bacon.

2. Place 4 donuts on top, adding scoops of ice cream and sprinkles of candied bacon on each one. Add a smaller layer of donuts, ice cream, and candied bacon on top until the cake is topped with the last donut, 1 scoop of ice cream, and a sprinkling of candied bacon.

3. It can be stored, tightly wrapped in plastic wrap, in the freezer for up to 3 days.

TIP: Instead of making the donuts from scratch, buy a dozen maple bacon donuts from your favorite donut shop. To make a showstopping donut cake, use two dozen donuts and add colorful sprinkles.

COOKIE BUTTER LOVERS' ICE CREAM CUPCAKES

MAKES 24 ice cream cupcakes | PREP TIME: 30 minutes, plus overnight to freeze | COOK TIME: 20 minutes

If you've never tasted cookie butter before, then let me introduce you to your next obsession. Cookie butter consists of crushed spice cookies blended to the consistency of peanut butter. It is so good, you'll find yourself eating it with a spoon. And when you make these ice cream cupcakes, I doubt there'll be any leftovers after you serve it.

For the cupcakes

2 cups all-purpose flour

½ teaspoon baking soda

½ teaspoon baking powder

¼ teaspoon salt

¼ teaspoon ground cinnamon

⅛ teaspoon ground nutmeg

½ cup unsalted butter, room temperature

¾ cup granulated sugar

¼ cup packed light brown sugar

1 cup creamy cookie butter

2 eggs, at room temperature

1 teaspoon vanilla extract

1½ cups whole milk

For the topping

½ cup crushed Biscoff cookies

For the no-churn ice cream

1 (14-ounce) can sweetened condensed milk

½ cup cookie butter

1 teaspoon vanilla extract

2 cups heavy cream

½ cup chopped Biscoff cookies

½ cup milk chocolate chips

To make the no-churn ice cream

1. In a small bowl, mix together the sweetened condensed milk, cookie butter, and vanilla extract. Set aside.

2. Whisk the heavy cream in a stand mixer on medium-high speed until it forms stiff peaks.

CONTINUED

3. Add the sweetened condensed milk mixture to the whipped cream and mix on medium-high speed until thick. Fold in the chopped cookies and chocolate chips, pour into an airtight container, and freeze overnight.

To make the cupcakes

1. Preheat the oven to 350°F. Line two 12-cup cupcake tins with 24 cupcake liners. Set aside.

2. In a small bowl, whisk together the flour, baking soda, baking powder, salt, cinnamon, and nutmeg. Set aside.

3. In a stand mixer on medium-high, cream the butter, granulated sugar, and brown sugar until light and creamy. Add the cookie butter and mix until combined. Add the eggs and vanilla extract and mix until combined. Adjust the speed to low and add the flour mixture, alternating with the milk, until completely mixed.

4. Remove the bowl from the mixer and use a rubber spatula to ensure the ingredients are incorporated.

5. Fill the cupcake liners ⅔ full of batter and bake, one tin at a time, for 20 minutes, or until a toothpick inserted in the middle comes out clean. Transfer the cupcakes to a wire rack to cool completely.

6. Store the cupcakes in an airtight container at room temperature.

To construct the cupcakes

When ready to serve, place a scoop of ice cream on top of each cupcake and sprinkle with crushed Biscoff cookies. These are best if made to order.

TIP: Cookie butter can be found next to the peanut butter at most grocery stores. It's sometimes called speculoos or Biscoff cookie butter. There are creamy and crunchy varieties of cookie butter, so try out both varieties.

SPRINKLE EXPLOSION ICE CREAM CAKE

MAKES **8 slices** | PREP TIME: **45 minutes, plus overnight to chill and overnight plus 1 hour 30 minutes to freeze** | COOK TIME: **35 minutes**

It's hard not to smile at any dessert covered in rainbow sprinkles! This fun cake is perfect for any party or celebration, especially with its layer of colorful vanilla ice cream.

For the cake

Nonstick cooking spray

3⅓ cups all-purpose flour

1 teaspoon baking powder

½ teaspoon baking soda

¼ teaspoon ground nutmeg

¼ teaspoon salt

2 cups granulated sugar

1 cup unsalted butter, melted

1½ cups whole milk, at room temperature

2 eggs, at room temperature

½ cup vanilla Greek yogurt, at room temperature

1 tablespoon vanilla extract

1 cup rainbow sprinkles

For the ice cream

3 cups heavy cream

1 cup whole milk

½ cup granulated sugar

½ cup light corn syrup

½ teaspoon salt

2½ teaspoons vanilla extract

1 cup rainbow sprinkles

For the frosting

1½ cups unsalted butter, cut into pieces

5 cups powdered sugar

2½ teaspoons vanilla extract

2 tablespoons heavy cream

½ teaspoon salt

For the topping

1 cup rainbow sprinkles

To make the ice cream

1. In a medium pot over medium heat, mix together the heavy cream, milk, sugar, corn syrup, and salt and bring the mixture to a simmer, stirring until the sugar dissolves. Remove from the heat and stir in the vanilla extract. Transfer the mixture to a bowl, cover with plastic wrap, and refrigerate overnight. Place the ice cream freeze bowl into the freezer overnight.

CONTINUED

2. Pour the chilled mixture into a 1½-quart ice cream maker and process according to the manufacturer's directions. Five minutes before the churning ends, add the sprinkles.

3. Line two 8-inch round cake pans with plastic wrap.

4. Divide the ice cream between the pans, cover them with plastic wrap, and freeze overnight.

To make the cake

1. Preheat the oven to 350°F. Line the bottom of three 8-inch round cake pans with parchment paper and spray the pans with cooking spray. Set aside.

2. In a medium bowl, whisk the flour, baking powder, baking soda, nutmeg, and salt.

3. In a large bowl, whisk together the sugar and butter until combined and gritty in texture. Add the milk and whisk until incorporated. Add the eggs, one a time, mixing thoroughly after each one. Whisk in the yogurt and vanilla extract until incorporated.

4. Slowly add the flour mixture and mix until combined. Gently fold the sprinkles into the batter until well distributed.

5. Remove the bowl from the mixer and use a rubber spatula to ensure the ingredients are incorporated.

6. Divide the batter equally among the three cake pans and bake for 20 minutes, or until a toothpick inserted in the middle comes out clean. Let cool in the pan for 10 minutes before transferring to a wire rack to finish cooling completely.

7. Store the cakes in an airtight container at room temperature for up to 3 days.

To make the frosting

1. In a stand mixer on medium-high speed, beat the butter for 5 to 7 minutes, until pale in color. Adjust the speed to low, add 2 cups of powdered sugar, and mix until incorporated. Add 2 teaspoons of vanilla extract and mix until combined.

2. Add 2 more cups of powdered sugar and mix until incorporated. Adjust the speed to medium-high and beat for 3 minutes.

3. Add the remaining 1 cup of powdered sugar, heavy cream, salt, and the remaining ½ teaspoon of vanilla extract and beat until incorporated. Adjust the speed to medium-high and beat for another 5 minutes.

To construct the cake

1. Place one layer of cake upside down on a cake plate. Add an ice cream layer and top with a second layer of cake. Add the second layer of ice cream and top with the third layer of cake.

2. Frost the top and sides of the cake. Pour the sprinkles evenly over the top, gently pressing them into the frosting.

3. Place the cake in the freezer to set for 30 minutes before covering tightly with plastic wrap and freezing for at least 1 hour until ready to serve.

4. Store leftovers, tightly covered in plastic wrap, in the freezer for 3 to 5 days.

TIP: Homemade frosting tastes a million times better than anything you can buy at the store. Using fresh, high-quality butter and cream is key to making a delicious buttercream, as is the vanilla extract you use. I prefer Rodelle Pure Vanilla Extract and I use their extracts exclusively in all my recipes.

THE GINGERBREAD MAN EATS ICE CREAM CAKE FOR BREAKFAST

MAKES **8 servings** | PREP TIME: **40 minutes, plus overnight to freeze** | COOK TIME: **30 minutes**

After one bite of these spicy gingerbread ice cream pancakes, I yearn for cool weather, scarves, and a roaring fireplace. But don't just eat them in the winter—they are great anytime. No butter or syrup is needed to top these pancakes when you have brown butter ice cream.

For the pancakes

3 cups all-purpose flour
½ cup packed light brown sugar
¼ cup granulated sugar
1 tablespoon baking powder
1 tablespoon ground cinnamon
1 teaspoon ground cloves
¾ teaspoon ground allspice
¼ teaspoon ground anise
½ teaspoon ground ginger
½ teaspoon ground nutmeg
¼ teaspoon ground coriander
¼ teaspoon ground cardamom
¼ teaspoon salt
2 cups whole milk
¼ cup honey
¼ cup molasses (not blackstrap)
2 eggs
¼ cup canola oil
1 teaspoon vanilla extract
Nonstick cooking spray (optional)

For the no-churn ice cream

½ cup butter
1 (14-ounce) can sweetened
   condensed milk
1 teaspoon vanilla extract
2 cups heavy cream

For the topping

½ cup crushed ginger snaps

To make the no-churn ice cream

1. In a medium pot over medium heat, melt the butter. Cook for 5 to 7 minutes, until the butter foams, turns golden brown, and smells slightly nutty. Remove from the heat and pour into a bowl, scraping all the brown bits into the bowl, and let cool.

2. Stir the sweetened condensed milk and vanilla extract into the cooled butter and set aside.

3. Whip the heavy cream in a stand mixer on medium-high speed until it forms stiff peaks. Mix in the sweetened condensed milk mixture on medium-high speed until thick. Transfer to an airtight container and freeze overnight.

To make the pancakes

1. In a large bowl, whisk together the flour, brown sugar, granulated sugar, baking powder, cinnamon, cloves, allspice, anise, ginger, nutmeg, coriander, cardamom, and salt. Add the milk, honey, molasses, eggs, oil, and vanilla and mix until combined.

2. Let the mixture rest for 5 minutes as you preheat a griddle on the stovetop over medium heat. Butter or spray the griddle with cooking spray, if not using a nonstick pan. Spoon ½ cup of batter onto the griddle for each pancake. When bubbles form on top of the pancake, flip it over and continue to cook for a few more minutes, until cooked through and browned. Place the pancakes on a plate and store in the microwave oven to stay warm.

3. To serve, place a pancake on a plate, top with a scoop of ice cream, and sprinkle the crushed gingersnaps over the top. Eat immediately.

4. Store leftover pancakes, tightly wrapped in plastic wrap, at room temperature for 1 to 2 days, or in the freezer.

TIP: Make your own gingerbread spice. Whisk together 4 tablespoons ground cinnamon, 1 tablespoon ground cloves, 1 tablespoon ground allspice, 1 teaspoon ground anise, 1 teaspoon ground ginger, ½ teaspoon ground nutmeg, ½ teaspoon ground coriander, and ½ teaspoon ground cardamom. Store in an airtight container for up to 6 months. Use 1 tablespoon of the gingerbread spice in place of all the spices in the pancake recipe.

Toppings and Decorations

My favorite part of eating ice cream is picking out what topping (or *toppings*) I'm going to use. The flavor of ice cream (and my mood) will usually determine what toppings I use, and let's face it: Life is too short to eat plain ice cream! Here are a few of my favorite toppings:

Chocolate Chips (of all varieties): dark chocolate chips, semi-sweet chocolate chips, milk chocolate chips, mini chocolate chips, white chocolate chips, butterscotch chips, and cinnamon chips. You can never go wrong with chocolate, and it's safe to say most people have a bag of chocolate chips stashed somewhere in their pantry. I like to put mini chocolate chips on top of my ice cream because then you can get more chocolate in each bite.

Sauces: The thicker the sauce, the better, in my opinion. Hot fudge sauce, caramel sauce, salted caramel, butterscotch sauce, and marshmallow crème . . . Buy premade sauces at the store or make your own. I like to heat sauces in the microwave for a few seconds before adding on top of my ice cream.

Spreads: Think peanut butter, Nutella, and cookie butter to name a few. There are so many different flavored nut butters out there to experiment with and they make for quick and easy ice cream toppings. Add a few spoonfuls of your desired "butter" into a bowl, microwave for 5 to 10 seconds, and immediately pour onto your ice cream to enjoy.

Fruit: Fresh fruit, such as strawberries, blueberries, bananas, and pineapple make for healthy and delicious ice cream toppings. Or, go for even more flavor and use canned pie filling over the ice cream: Apple pie filling, cherry pie filling, or strawberry pie filling are all great.

Sprinkles: Rainbow sprinkles and chocolate sprinkles add a nice "crunch." Jimmies are the best type of sprinkles to use because they don't bleed their color out into the ice cream. The larger candy sprinkles are a good option, too.

Cookies: Store-bought cookies and homemade cookies are some of my favorite ice cream toppings. Oreos, Chips Ahoy!, and Nutter Butters are just a few options to crumble onto ice cream. There's also nothing better than a warm, home-baked chocolate chip cookie on top. I include graham crackers in this category as well.

I love their texture when you crush them and sprinkle onto ice cream. Another option is to buy premade graham cracker crusts from the baking aisle and crush them into pieces to top your ice cream.

Nuts: Pistachios, almonds, peanuts, pecans, and walnuts are great places to start. Toast the nuts to get a richer flavor before adding to your ice cream. You can also melt chocolate chips in the microwave and toss the nuts in the melted chocolate before adding to your ice cream.

Chocolate Candies: M&M's, Snickers, peanut butter cups, and Milky Ways—I could go crazy listing all of the chocolate candy options for topping ice cream, but really it comes down to the ice cream flavor. Chop the candy into small pieces or buy mini candy bars.

Gummy Candies: Gummy bears, sour gummy worms, or any other gummy variety are great for topping vanilla ice cream or tart- and fruit-flavored ice creams. I like the way their texture changes after sitting in the freezing ice cream.

Cookie Dough: Use premade cookie dough from the refrigerator section at the grocery store, or make your own safe-to-eat raw cookie dough by mixing together 2⅓ cup heat-treated all-purpose flour (baked at 350° for 5 minutes), ⅔ cup light brown sugar, 8 tablespoons unsalted butter at room temperature, 1 (14-ounce) can sweetened condensed milk, 1 teaspoon vanilla extract, a pinch of salt, and ½ cup mini chocolate chips. Store in the refrigerator.

Serving Sizes

The serving sizes listed in the recipes are suggestions only and are a great base to gauge how many people the cake will feed. You may get more servings from a cake, or less, depending on how big or small you cut the slices or squares. For cakes that are three layers of cake and two layers of ice cream, a smaller slice goes a long way. When serving cake to my family I just usually ask whether they want a big slice or a small slice (you don't want to lose out on leftovers due to uneaten cake!). The cupcakes are single serving, as are the cheesecake cups and donut sandwiches. One scoop of ice cream on the cupcakes, cheesecake cups, and donut sandwiches is average, but I always offer an extra scoop of ice cream on the side for people, too. The amount of servings you get from the pancake ice cream creations is dependent upon how big the pancakes are and how many pancakes a person wants.

Measurement Conversions

	US STANDARD	US STANDARD (OUNCES)	METRIC (APPROXIMATE)
VOLUME EQUIVALENTS (LIQUID)	2 tablespoons	1 fl. oz.	30 mL
	¼ cup	2 fl. oz.	60 mL
	½ cup	4 fl. oz.	120 mL
	1 cup	8 fl. oz.	240 mL
	1½ cups	12 fl. oz.	355 mL
	2 cups or 1 pint	16 fl. oz.	475 mL
	4 cups or 1 quart	32 fl. oz.	1 L
	1 gallon	128 fl. oz.	4 L
VOLUME EQUIVALENTS (DRY)	⅛ teaspoon	————	0.5 mL
	¼ teaspoon	————	1 mL
	½ teaspoon	————	2 mL
	¾ teaspoon	————	4 mL
	1 teaspoon	————	5 mL
	1 tablespoon	————	15 mL
	¼ cup	————	59 mL
	⅓ cup	————	79 mL
	½ cup	————	118 mL
	⅔ cup	————	156 mL
	¾ cup	————	177 mL
	1 cup	————	235 mL
	2 cups or 1 pint	————	475 mL
	3 cups	————	700 mL
	4 cups or 1 quart	————	1 L
	½ gallon	————	2 L
	1 gallon	————	4 L
WEIGHT EQUIVALENTS	½ ounce	————	15 g
	1 ounce	————	30 g
	2 ounces	————	60 g
	4 ounces	————	115 g
	8 ounces	————	225 g
	12 ounces	————	340 g
	16 ounces or 1 pound	————	455 g

	FAHRENHEIT (F)	CELSIUS (C) (APPROXIMATE)
OVEN TEMPERATURES	250°F	120°F
	300°F	150°C
	325°F	180°C
	375°F	190°C
	400°F	200°C
	425°F	220°C
	450°F	230°C

Resources

The following are brand names mentioned in this book: Cuisinart Ice Cream Maker, KitchenAid stand mixer, Rodelle Gourmet Vanilla Extract, Mars, Nestlé and Hershey candies, General Mills cereal, Nutella, Lotus Biscoff cookie butter and cookies, Breyers Ice Cream, Ben & Jerry's Ice Cream, and Nabisco cookies.

References

Foster, Kelli. *"The 4 Essential Ice Cream Bases You Should Know"* thekitchn.com. Updated May 1, 2019. https://www.thekitchn.com /the-4-bases-to-know-for-making-homemade-ice-cream-221723.

Laperruque, Emma. *"How to Make Ice Cream"* food52.com. July 12, 2019. https://food52.com/blog/24335-how-to-make-ice-cream.

Index

Acknowledgments

First and foremost, I want to thank my husband James and son Ethan for being patient and understanding as I worked day and night on this book, and for listening to me talk only about ice cream and cakes for weeks on end. They're my best taste testers and I appreciate all the calories they consumed during recipe testing!

Second, I would like to thank my mom, dad, sister, brother-in-law, and two nieces for giving me a lifetime of memories and love that inspired a lot of these ice cream cake creations. A huge thanks to my friend and fellow blogger GiGi Ashworth. Without her, this cookbook dream of mine would never have become a reality.

And last, but not least, Callisto Media and Natasha Yglesias for bringing my dreams of an ice cream cake cookbook to life! I appreciate all their hard work, edits, encouragement, guidance, and patience.

About the Author

Kelly Mikolich is a self-taught baker who learned everything she knows from her mother, two years of high school home economics class, obsessively watching Food Network, and reading cookbooks. After experimenting in the kitchen and making different desserts, Kelly started her blog *Kelly Lynn's Sweets and Treats* as a way of documenting the recipes she created while sharing those recipes with family, friends, and blog readers. She works a full-time job in the public safety sector and is known at work for the treats she brings in to share. Kelly lives in the Central Valley of California with her husband, James, and son, Ethan.

CPSIA information can be obtained
at www.ICGtesting.com
Printed in the USA
LVHW022150271219
641909LV00001B/1

9 781641 527262